Latasha

and the

KIDD ON KEYS

ALSO BY MICHAEL SCOTTO

In collaboration with Lincoln Learning Solutions

Latasha and the Little Red Tornado
Postcards from Pismo

The Tales of Midlandia series including:

Be a Buddy, Not a Bully
Builda the Re-Bicycler
Just Flash
Nothing but the Truth
The Pirate Koostoe

Latasha

and the

KIDD ON KEYS

A novel by Michael Scotto

Illustrations by Evette Gabriel

LINCOLN
LEARNING
SOLUTIONS

© 2016 Lincoln Learning Solutions

294 Massachusetts Avenue
Rochester, PA 15074
All rights reserved.

Visit us on the web at
http://www.lincolnlearningsolutions.org.

Midlandia® is a registered trademark of
Lincoln Learning Solutions.

Edited by Ashley Mortimer
Typography by D. Kent Kerr

ISBN-13: 978-1-938165-07-8

Printed in the USA.

First printing, March 2013.
Revised edition.

As always, for J & L, my family

Table of Contents

Prologue
1

Chapter One
Gifted – 7

Chapter Two
The Tangled Tree – 31

Chapter Three
New Dog – 53

Chapter Four
Common Grounds – 74

Chapter Five
Talent Pool – 91

Chapter Six
Kidd on Keys – 106

Chapter Seven
Ella's Anniversary – 132

Chapter Eight
The Lonely Dog Blues – 158

Chapter Nine
Secret Weapon – 175

Chapter Ten
Innovations, Conversations – 197

Chapter Eleven
The First Snow – 221

Chapter Twelve
Family-Only – 239

Prologue

It's always been a mystery how I wound up with Ella.

I know where Momma and I found her—that's no mystery at all. We'd plucked my dog from a roomful of yipping strays at the Lucky Paws animal shelter two summers back. I also know how Ella came to Lucky Paws. A dog catcher for the city had discovered her on the streets. To be more specific—and if I want to be a good writer, I've learned, I should always be specific—they'd found her in a parking lot out behind a Dairy Queen on the South Side of Pittsburgh. The store manager had caught her trying to steal leftover Blizzards from the garbage. Ella didn't have a collar or any tags, so he reported her to Animal Control.

Momma and I learned about that episode from the file folder that came with Ella, which is kind of like the permanent record you get in school. It also had her vaccination papers, her weight (nineteen pounds then, fifty-four pounds now), and her fur color—as if you could possibly miss the short red hairs she leaves on every surface she touches.

But everything that came before the Dairy Queen is a blank. The shelter didn't know how long Ella had been on the streets, just that it had been a long time. They could only guess her birth month—April, they picked. They didn't even bother guessing what breed Ella is. The shelter put down "mix," which might as well have been "?" I understand why the folks at

Lucky Paws did that, though. Each part of Ella looks like it came from a different kind of dog.

But here is the biggest mystery of all. I just don't get who could have abandoned Ella in the first place. I can't understand how someone once looked at this mixed-up little cutie and thought, *I don't want her*.

I wanted Ella the moment I met her. I remember every detail about that day. It was Saturday, June thirteenth, and I had just graduated from first grade the day before. At my school, Cedarville Elementary, that's the year students start to get letter grades on their report cards, and I'm proud to report that I had received all "A"s!

"Put on your sneakers, my straight-A star," Momma told me that morning.

"Where are we going?" I asked. *Not far*, I remember hoping. It wasn't too hot yet, but it was very sticky—the kind of day where it seems like the weather can't decide if it's spring or summer and your hair shoots off your head like broken bedsprings. The only traveling I wanted to do was through my new stack of library books, next to the living room fan.

But when Momma answered, I forgot all about Chewandswallow and Klickitat Street. I must have forgotten how to close my mouth, too, because Momma laughed and said, "Pick your jaw up off the floor, silly. Let's go before the day really heats up."

I knew Momma had always had dogs growing up. But for most of the walk over, I simply refused to believe that we were actually going to adopt one.

"Can we really afford a puppy?" I asked. We didn't have a lot of money then. We still don't, really, but back then, when Momma was a hotel cleaning lady instead of a nursing aide, we had even less.

Momma glanced down at me with a grin. "That's a Momma problem," she said, "not a Latasha problem." That was her way of telling me, *I've got it covered*.

"And Mrs. O really said it was okay," I said skeptically. Mrs. Okocho is our landlady, an old Nigerian woman who lives on the first floor of our house.

Momma gave me a believe-it-or-not nod.

"But where will it go to the bathroom?" I asked. We only had a tiny square of grass behind the house. And as for the front yard…I couldn't imagine that a serious gardener like Mrs. Okocho would let a dog make number two on the same *block* as her flowerbeds.

"There's an old saying," Momma replied evenly. "'Never look a gift horse in the mouth.'"

I had no idea what gift horses had to do with dogs, but Momma's tone convinced me to hold my tongue the rest of the walk over.

When we came into Lucky Paws, the girl at the front desk led us back to see the holding area. That was where all of the dogs lived.

The holding area was lined with grated pens on either side. I held Momma's hand as I looked at each dog. Some were panting, tongues out like pink streamers. Others were barking. Others were pawing at their cage doors. I felt like Goldilocks from that fairy tale. None of the dogs seemed just right.

But then I spotted her. In a pen near the back of the room, I saw a bony red puppy lying on a folded-up Pittsburgh Pirates beach towel. "Poor thing ate her bed," the handler explained.

That ratty towel with the nibbled-on hemline was all she had; no toys, no nametag—even her tail looked as if she'd borrowed it from some other, much larger, dog. Something about her wide, quivery brown eyes made me want to pet her and tell her everything was okay. I asked the handler to open her gate.

The moment the handler unfastened the latch, the sickly puppy sprang with a sudden burst of life. She shot out of the pen, paws clicking, tail whipping against her sides, and she leapt chest-high a foot in front of me. Momma gasped and stepped back, but I reached out and caught the puppy in my arms. I felt her ribs against my forearms, her heart pounding. And when she licked my nose, I knew inside that she was mine and I was hers.

I named her right then, after a jazz singer Momma liked to play for me. I whispered her name like a prayer into the fur on her neck: three words…

Chapter One

Gifted

"Ella Fitzgerald Gandy," I warned, pointing my pencil at her.

I was sitting at the kitchen table in our house on Graham Street. A drawing of half a dog waited in front of me, aching to be finished—if only a certain little red beast would sit still for it!

At the moment, though, Ella had no interest in posing. She was intent on eating her own tail. She kept hopping up with her forepaws and twirling her bendy body on her rear leg, like a pinwheel in a wind storm.

"Please sit," I instructed. I hoped that I sounded firm and in charge, and not nervous like I really was. Ricky Jenkins's birthday party was less than three hours away, and this gift of his wasn't even finished, let alone wrapped and ribboned.

You might think, since I was making Ricky's present on the day of his party, that I hadn't put a lot of thought into it. But you'd be so wrong that it's not even funny. I'd been thinking about Ricky's present for a whole month, ever since we had finished third grade. I'd figured that it would be easy to pick the perfect gift. After all, Ricky isn't just some boy who lives across the street from me. He's my best friend—my best *human* friend, that is. But Ricky turned out to be very difficult to shop for.

Part of the trouble was that Ricky is a boy. Who knows what silly things a boy is going to like from one week to the next? A boy's brain is like one of those Magic 8 Balls. He'll think one thing's his favorite thing in the world, but if you give him one good shake, he'll completely change his mind.

On top of the whole boy issue, Ricky wasn't having just any birthday. He was turning ten. You'd never guess it by his height or his goofball sense of humor, but Ricky is a full six months older than me. He's actually the oldest kid in our grade. That's because he did kindergarten twice—"because I loooooved nap time!" he says.

But the hardest part wasn't that Ricky is a boy or that he was turning ten. The real problem was that best friends have to get each other the best presents. It's basically a rule. But every time I thought up an awesome present for Ricky, he either already had it or Momma and I couldn't afford it. Or both, like when I thought of getting him a signed jersey of his favorite Pittsburgh Steeler, Casey Hampton.

After a lot of thinking, I realized that I did have one thing that Ricky didn't: Ella. Ricky loves Ella almost as much as I do. He thinks it's awesome that she's a mutt and that she only has three legs and is a tripod dog. He even invited Ella to his party today. She got her own invitation and everything—which, of course, she ate.

I knew that Ricky's dream was to have a dog of his own, but I wasn't about to give Ella to him for his birthday. So I did the next best thing: I wrote about all the fun times he's had with her. To be extra creative, I pretended that I was Ella and wrote it from her point of view. I called it *Wild Days with Ricky*.

Which I would've gladly written down, if I could ever finish this drawing! "You are ruining your portrait," I scolded as Ella spun.

"Portrait?" asked Momma from the doorway. She was fastening her pink nametag to her scrubs. Momma usually didn't work on Saturdays, but she liked to pick up an extra shift at Children's Hospital whenever she could. "I thought you wrote Ricky a story."

"I wrote him a book," I corrected. "This is the cover. You can't have a book without a cover."

Momma slipped past my whirling pup and

fetched some cold cuts from the fridge. "I don't know where it comes from," she said. "So gifted…"

I smiled as I waited for the rest of the sentence. "And talented," Momma added as she fixed herself a sandwich for her lunch break.

All this summer, Momma had been going out of her way to call me "gifted and talented." She'd started it at the end of school. That was when Mr. Harvey— my third-grade teacher and the coolest grown-up in all of Cedarville Elementary—invited me to join our school's Gifted and Talented Club. Its nickname is the Talent Pool, and Mr. Harvey runs it. The club is all fourth and fifth graders, and it meets in his classroom once a week after school.

When Momma had started her whole "gifted and talented" kick, I'd thought it would get old fast—but it hadn't yet. What *had* worn out its welcome, though, was Ella's bad behavior. She'd abandoned her tail-chasing and was now wiggling in front of my shins, begging me to play.

"Sit," I told her again. I just knew that I should have drawn this picture while Ella was asleep. My girl is the cutest sleeper. She kicks her back paw off to the side and stretches her forepaws ahead, crossing them like a dainty little lady.

When Ella's awake, she is anything but dainty.

As I tried to sketch her floppy beagle ears, she was butting her sinewy shoulder into my calf so that I might stand up. *Sinewy* is this nifty word I found in my pocket dictionary. It means muscular, but not like a weightlifter—more like a sprinter. I love finding just the right word. Momma might say it is both a *gift* and a *talent* of mine.

"No play," I told Ella, rooting my foot to the kitchen floor. I usually loved our playtimes together, but I could almost hear the stove's clock ticking toward party time.

Momma zipped her roast beef sandwich in a plastic baggie. "You try her usual bribe?" she asked.

Momma meant Teddy Snacks, which are a tasty, bear-shaped cracker that Ella will basically do anything to get. I shot Momma a grumbly look that I hoped said, *Of course, that was the first thing I tried!*

She shrugged her eyebrows. "Just trying to help," she said, and she turned to pack her lunch into a brown paper bag.

"It almost worked," I said, feeling guilty for my attitude. "I just couldn't hold the treat up, hold the paper in place, and draw all at the same time. I need three arms."

"Or an assistant," Momma suggested.

I pushed my pencil aside. "You have time?"

Ella, who'd been whipping back and forth to watch us talk, turned to pant in Momma's direction.

"Not me," Momma replied.

I frowned. She meant Mrs. Okocho downstairs. "No way," I said. "Not today."

It's not that I don't like Mrs. Okocho. I actually like her a lot. She's more than our landlady. She's like the grandmother I never had—even if she does get cranky about Ella sometimes. But today was supposed to be a special day. Today, Momma's work started at eleven, Ricky's party started at one—and for the two hours in between, for the first time ever, Momma was letting me stay in the apartment by myself! I'd been fighting for that privilege for a year, and I wasn't about to ruin it by inviting Mrs. Okocho up.

Momma pointed two fingers at Ella and me. "You make a heck of a pair," she said. "Stubborn One and Stubborn Two. C'mere."

I set down my pencil and went over to Momma. She smoothed a curl of hair back on my head. She had that *Aw, my little baby* look in her eyes, and I worried that she would change her mind and send me downstairs to be babysat. But then she asked me, "What are the rules?"

I smiled in relief. I'd practiced this test in my head

dozens of times. "No answering the door," I began. "No using the stove. No phone calls."

"And tell Mrs. O when you leave for the party," Momma said.

"I will," I promised. I noticed that the room had gone quiet. That was rarely a good sign with Ella.

"And go straight to Ricky's and then straight home," Momma added.

"Straight across the street and straight home," I agreed. I looked back and spotted my pup sitting near the table. Now that I'd stopped trying to draw her, she was perfectly still, right down to her tail. It just figured.

"Go ahead," said Momma, slinging her bag over her shoulder. "Finish your present."

I gave Momma an extra big hug. "Be good!" I told her.

"Hey!" she said in mock surprise. "That's my line."

Momma kissed me quickly on the crown of my head, opened the door, and left for work.

I waited a few seconds, listening as the hall stairs creaked with Momma's footsteps. I heard her knock on Mrs. Okocho's door and let her know that I was upstairs. Finally, the front door downstairs opened, then shut.

I couldn't hold it in any more. I pumped my

fists and wiggled my hips. I didn't care how silly I looked—I had the apartment to myself!

"*Home, home on the range*," I sang, spinning around on the ball of my foot. "*Where a girl and her little dog—*"

As soon as I faced Ella, she popped up and tore out of the kitchen. My arms dropped to my sides. "Aw, girl!" I moaned. I followed her into the living room just in time to see her leap onto the couch, spin around, and dash toward my bedroom.

"No zoomies!" I pleaded as I heard the books on my bedside table crash to the floor.

Ella bounded back into the living room. "Careful!" I winced as she banged her left hip into our little coffee table. I always felt nervous and a bit guilty when Ella ran her scar into things.

It didn't faze her, though. Ella leapt again and bashed into the couch like she was at football practice. The couch slid half a foot toward me. I leaned over it and wrapped my arms around the wriggling beast. "We have to finish this present, or else…" I struggled to keep my grip as I thought up a threat. Only one thing came to mind: *Or else we'll both be terrible friends.*

In the kitchen, the phone rang. I looked away from Ella and she wriggled free.

The phone rang again. I knew that I wasn't supposed to answer it—but I really wanted to know who was calling. It rang a third time. Was it a telemarketer? Or was it something important? Maybe it was Momma with an emergency.

As Ella wreaked more havoc in my bedroom, I went for the phone. I took a deep breath and answered.

"Gandy residence," I said with a smile.

"You are not supposed to answer," said an accented voice. It was Mrs. Okocho.

"Then why did you call at all?" I demanded. I hate being set up.

Mrs. Okocho paused. "Your mama says you are making a portrait," she finally said. "But it sounds like you are making a war zone."

My skin tingled as I imagined what Ella's rampage sounded like downstairs. "Sorry," was all I could say.

"I will come and help," Mrs. Okocho said.

I heard Ella dash back into the living room, growling like a car engine. I'd really wanted to handle this myself, but there was no time to be prideful. "Thank you," I replied.

"Then it is settled!" our landlady declared. "I will bring for us a moofin to eat."

"A moofin?" I asked with dread. Was that one of

those smelly Nigerian stews she was always cooking?

"Yes! I went this morning to the bakery, for something to have with my coffee," she said. "This blueberry moofin is bigger than my foot!"

"Oh, a *muffin*," I said. Mrs. Okocho's accent made certain words sound so unusual. I loved that about her.

"See you in a flash," she said. We hung up the phone, and moments later I heard the hall stairs groan beneath Mrs. Okocho's bunny slippers.

An hour later, Mrs. Okocho was still upstairs bribing Ella to sit still for her portrait. Mrs. Okocho had not wanted to risk being licked by Ella—"Think of the germs, child!"—so she'd refused to hold the Teddy Snack in her fingers. But with a yardstick and a pack of dental floss that I hoped Momma wouldn't miss, I'd been able to devise a clever solution.

Mrs. Okocho sat on the couch dangling a Teddy Snack above Ella's head. I had tied dental floss around the snack's little ankle and then taped the dental floss to the yardstick, making it kind of like a fishing pole.

"Soon, my darling, soon," Mrs. Okocho told Ella as she shook the yardstick gently. She turned to me.

"Right?"

I nodded. I was so close to finishing! I'd drawn her broad mastiff chest and her stout pit bull forelegs. I was just working on her back half, which was long and lean like a greyhound's. I'd drawn her rear right leg, but there was one part that I couldn't decide on.

The trouble was this: Ella hadn't always had just three legs. When Ricky had first met her, she'd had all four. She lost her left hind leg nine months ago when she got away from me and ended up being hit by a car. The car broke Ella's leg. Dr. Vanderstam tried to do an operation to save it, but it was too badly hurt to ever heal right, so he'd had to take it off.

Ella doesn't miss her leg one bit, but I couldn't decide—should I draw her with three legs and her scar, or draw in the fourth leg that she had when Ricky first met her?

"You are upset," Mrs. Okocho observed. "What is your trouble?"

I told her what was bothering me.

"Draw her as she is now," she said. "Your Ella is very pretty, you know."

I smiled. Mrs. Okocho was goofy most times, but other times she knew just what to say. I finished the picture and carefully printed the book's title on it. Below that, I wrote: *by Ella Fitzgerald Gandy*.

"All finished!" I announced.

Mrs. Okocho lowered the Teddy Snack to Ella, who carefully broke it away from the dental floss and ate it.

"Good girl!" I said in surprise.

"Yes, yes," Mrs. Okocho said. And then she did something very unusual: she petted Ella's back. She did it lightly at first, like she thought it might feel gross, but then she petted her more firmly. "Very good girl." The sight of it made my insides all warm, like a drink of cocoa on a snow day.

Ella must have enjoyed it, too, because she spun around, put her paws on the couch, and licked Mrs. Okocho right on the face. The landlady let out a screech and bolted to her feet. "Oh, disgusting!" she cried, blinking rapidly. "Oh, the germs."

Mrs. Okocho waved her hands at me. "Child, child, fetch me the *roobing* alcohol."

Wouldn't you know that after all my fuss and worry, Ella and I still ended up being the first to arrive at Ricky's. I didn't mind, though. It gave us time to talk before Ricky had to pay attention to all of his other friends. "She's been so great with Ella," I told him. "I've got to do something extra nice for her."

"You could dust her apartment," he suggested.

"Never again," I said. I'd tried to dust for Mrs. Okocho once, in exchange for a ride to the library. "That lady has two feather dusters—one to dust her furniture, and another to dust off the first duster."

"Crazy," Ricky said. "Go get it!" He hurled a tooth-marked Frisbee across the yard and Ella raced after it. Ricky's yard was her favorite outdoor place because it was all fenced in, which meant no leash. She liked it even better than Friendship Park down the road. Since Ella's accident, Ricky's parents had let her come here to play so that we didn't have to make the long walk there. And also, I think, so Ricky would quit asking for a dog of his own.

Ella launched herself like a pogo stick and caught the Frisbee in her mouth. "Good catch!" Ricky shouted. "Now, bring it back!"

Ella trotted away to the corner of the yard. She was great at the *go-get-it* part of playing Fetch—but awful at the *bring-it-back* part.

I grinned at the pup as she whipped the Frisbee from side to side in her mouth.

"Ricky?" Mrs. Jenkins called from the back door. "Help me set up the snack table." She was awkwardly holding a long folding table up by one corner.

Ricky turned heavily and slumped his shoulders.

"On my *birthday*?" he moaned. He might have turned double-digits, but it certainly hadn't changed him much.

I thought about giving him a quick punch in that ticklish spot on his side for whining, but I didn't like to get too feisty in front of Mrs. Jenkins. She's one of those ladies who always looks like she stepped off the cover of *Essence* magazine—so I try to be my most proper around her.

"Gosh, Ricky, show some dignity," I said. He threw me a smirk. "I can help you, Mrs. Jenkins!"

"Sweet music to my ears," she sighed.

I jogged to the sliding back door and grabbed the table's other end. Mrs. Jenkins and I carried it out to the grass together. "Can I ask you a favor?" I asked as we pulled out the table's legs.

"Sure, Latasha, what do you need?" Mrs. Jenkins replied.

"It's about my present for Ricky," I confided. "Can you make sure he opens it last?"

Mrs. Jenkins smiled. "Got something special, huh?"

We glanced over at Ricky, who was trying to wrestle the Frisbee away from Ella. "I can't throw if you don't let go," he was saying.

"It's one of a kind," I replied.

"Well," Mrs. Jenkins began, "let's play it by ear. Mr. Jenkins kind of wants *his* present to be the grand finale. But he's still out picking it up."

I had to admit, if anyone could edge me out for "best present," it was Mr. Jenkins. He worked as a lawyer at a firm downtown, and he always got cool things through his job, like box seats for the Steelers and tickets to plays.

Ricky's mom and I flipped the table onto its legs. "You go ahead and play," she told me. "I've got it from here."

Mrs. Jenkins went into the house and I returned to Ricky and my pup.

"I'd been wondering where your dad was," I said. Mr. Jenkins almost never missed things that mattered to Ricky. I'd been surprised that he wasn't home when we arrived. "Any idea what he's getting you?"

"I hope it's a drum set," Ricky said. "He tried to go today without me noticing, but I totally saw him take the SUV."

On top of being the year that you can join Gifted and Talented at our school, fourth grade is the year you get to join the band. Ricky really wanted to play the drums. He'd been scheming all summer to get a set. If Ricky's dad had finally given in, I was *definitely* okay with him going last.

"Jeez, I hope I'm not interrupting your date!" yelled a boy from the door.

I scowled. It was Ricky's dopey friend, Dante Preston. Ricky ruffled the fur on Ella's back. "Go get him!" he told her.

When Ella gets excited, she doesn't run to you— she swims. On Ricky's command, my pup wagged her tail frantically and did a wiggly, floppy skip toward Dante.

Dante's eyes bulged and he clung to the door handle. "Jenkins, c'mon," he cried, his voice cracking. "Don't!"

I almost felt bad for the kid, even with those "date" cracks he was always making. I clapped my hands and said, "Ella, come!"

Ella sniffed behind Dante's knees and then returned to me. Dante's shoulders sank in relief.

Mrs. Jenkins came to the door behind Dante with a pair of snack bowls. When she tapped on the glass, he yelped in surprise. Ricky doubled over in hysterics. Ella twirled on her hind leg.

Dante moved aside so Mrs. Jenkins could carry out the Doritos and Skittles. "Not cool, bro," he told Ricky. "I almost died, for real."

"I'll put her on her leash," I huffed. "Don't pee your pants."

That made Ricky lose it all over again. I saw Mrs. Jenkins raise an eyebrow at me as she walked back to the house and my cheeks got warm.

I clicked Ella's leash onto her collar. "She's really nice," I told Dante. "She just loves meeting people."

We heard the glass door slide open again, and out came another one of my old classmates, Darla Robinson. "Happy birthday, dear Ricky!" she sang.

Ella wiggled and tugged at her leash. I looked to Dante. "See?"

More kids arrived and the party got rolling. We played all kinds of games, like Tag and Back-to-Back Balloon Pop. We also had a three-legged race, which I didn't want to do at first because I thought Ricky was making a joke about Ella. But then I learned that a three-legged race is actually a real thing. It gets its name from the way the runners have to race in pairs, with one of each runner's legs tied to the other person's. I didn't do so well, because I got paired up with Darla. You have to work in perfect sync to win a three-legged race, but we each tried to lead the way.

After a while, Mrs. Jenkins brought the presents and yellow cake out and set them on the snack table. We all agreed to do the cake first in order to give Mr. Jenkins more time to get back with his present.

Everybody sang "Happy Birthday," but Ricky

seemed glum. "What's going on?" I asked while he cut the cake.

Ricky looked me. "He's going to miss the whole party."

"No way," I replied. "You'll see."

Ricky nodded and handed me a slice so huge that it barely fit on my plate.

"I can't eat all that cake!" I cried.

"It's not for you," Ricky retorted. "It's for her." Ella clipped my calves with her wagging tail.

We all ate our cake—don't worry, I only gave my pup one little bite—and then Ricky's mom carried out the presents. She set mine on the folding table first so that it would be on the bottom of the pile. I gripped Ella's leash. "This is going to be awesome," I whispered in her ear.

As Ricky opened his gifts, each guest called out which one they'd given. "That's mine!" yelled Darla as he grabbed a box wrapped in yellow-and-blue striped paper. Ricky tore off the paper to reveal a trivia board game.

"That's from me," called Dante as Ricky opened an envelope and pulled out a prepaid debit card. "So you can get whatever you want."

At some time during the gift opening, Ella finally ran out of steam and flopped down in the grass. I was getting more and more pumped, though. Ricky had gotten some cool presents, for sure—but mine would be the most unique.

Only a couple others' gifts and mine were left to open when we heard a familiar voice at the back door.

"I hope you didn't eat all the cake," Mr. Jenkins said. He was leaning around the side of the door frame, just a head and half of a chest.

"Dad!" Ricky shouted.

"Hi, Mr. Jenkins," a few of us said.

Mrs. Jenkins gave her husband a smooch on the temple. She peeked past him into the house. "Think we can hold off until we open the other presents?" she asked.

I hope so, I thought. I didn't know what could be in there—but Mrs. Jenkins sure looked excited when she saw it. Ella just shifted her head in my lap and huffed.

"Ooh, I don't know if it can wait," Mr. Jenkins replied, shooting Ricky a gleaming grin.

"What is it? What is it?" asked Ricky.

I couldn't see too well because the folding table was in my way. I craned my neck as Mr. Jenkins stepped slowly out of the house.

When Ricky saw his present, he didn't even say words. He just sprinted over to his parents, repeating over and over, "Oh…oh…" He hugged his dad tight, right in front of everybody.

Then he knelt down to pet his brand-new puppy.

The dog was gray—almost blue—with oversized paws, wrinkly knees, and a head shaped like a road worker's shovel. "He's a Great Dane," Mr. Jenkins said.

"He's the best Dane ever!" Ricky cried, hugging the puppy. His parents squatted down to welcome their new family member.

I felt a whole swarm of things at the same time. Part of me was so happy for my friend, who had all but given up on getting a dog of his own. And part of me wanted to hide my present for Ricky, which didn't feel like such a big deal anymore. And another part of me was eager to plan some play dates for Ella and this new pup.

But there was another thing, too, underneath all that. It was a feeling I have sometimes when I watch all of the Jenkinses having a great family moment together. I couldn't find the right word for it. It was like my heart was being held underwater. I closed my eyes and scratched the scruff of Ella's neck, hoping it would go away before anyone noticed me.

"Latasha!" Ricky said. I opened my eyes and saw him peering through the crowd of kids. "Bring Ella over!"

I smiled too hard at him, and then moved Ella's head so I could stand. I jingled her collar. "Come on, sleepy," I said. She lifted herself and we walked together around the table. I might have felt a bit gloomy, but I really was glad that Ella could make a new friend.

But she didn't make a new friend. She did something I'd never seen her do before. The instant we rounded the table's edge, the fur on Ella's back spiked up like a mohawk. Her lip curled and she let out the scariest snarl I've ever heard. Then she rushed so hard at Ricky's dog that her nails tore chunks from

the grass. Guests leapt out of the way. The Great Dane tensed up and growled. I yanked Ella's leash and Mr. Jenkins pulled back on theirs.

"Ella, no!" I screamed. Ella looped her leash around a table leg and flipped the whole thing, smashing cake and snacks and presents in a messy pile. I wrapped the leash around my hand, praying she wouldn't pull free. When I was sure of my grip, I pulled sharply and marched us off. I heard Ricky call my name, but I was too ashamed to look back. I just dragged Ella away at top speed—away from the party, across the yard, and out the side gate without even a glance.

Chapter Two
The Tangled Tree

"Why did you do that?" I asked Ella. I'd been asking that question for hours—sometimes in frustration, sometimes in tears. In one snarling move, my pup had threatened Ricky's dog, wrecked his party, and probably ended our friendship.

All of that was bad enough. But the worst part was that I couldn't talk to anyone else about it. If I told Momma what had happened, she might not trust Ella to sleep in my room anymore. If I told Mrs.

Okocho, forget about my room—she might not want my pup in the house at all.

And that was everybody I trusted. The only one I could talk to was Ella, even though she'd caused all of this trouble and made me so upset that I could barely look at her.

The pup didn't have any answers, though. She was curled up on my bed, tucked into a round, red lump. She did that when I got upset, because she knew I thought it was cute. How could a dog that knew how to cheer me up and snuggle just right to keep my toes warm at bedtime also be a mean, growly beast?

The thought kept me up that night, and it stayed in my mind while Momma and I ran our Sunday errands. It didn't take long for Momma to notice.

"What's dragging you down?" she asked me as we climbed off the city bus.

"These canned veggies," I said, hefting my doubled-up plastic grocery bag. "They weigh a ton."

"Really, honey," Momma said. "You haven't seemed like yourself since last night."

I shrugged coolly.

"Latasha," she said. "What kind of family are we?"

"A no-secrets family," I replied. That was a deal Momma and I had made this year. We started it because I always try to act tough and grown-up, even when I'm upset—kind of like right now, actually.

Most times, I think it's a great idea to be "no-secrets" with Momma. Most times.

I focused on the road. If I looked Momma in the eyes, I wouldn't be able to keep it in. "I'm just thinking of a story," I replied.

"Well, then," Momma said, shifting her grocery bags in her hand. "I'll leave my gifted and talented girl to her thoughts." We walked up the hill toward our block. "If you want to talk, though…about your story…I'm right here."

I glanced at Momma without turning. I felt a little bad being dishonest, but it was only a half-lie. I actually was thinking of a story: Ella's story. When I really thought about it, there were so many important parts that I didn't know.

I didn't know what she'd been through before we'd adopted her. Maybe she'd had a fight with a Great Dane when she was living on the streets and Ricky's dog reminded her of it.

I also didn't know where Ella had gone the time she got away from me last fall.

The time you let her go, my brain told me. *The time you let her get—*

I blinked my eyes a few times, like I was flicking the lights on and off in my head. I couldn't start beating myself up about Ella's accident. I still feel guilty about it sometimes, and Momma says that's normal—but last year's accident and yesterday's freak-out probably had nothing to do with each other.

We entered the apartment to the usual Ella greeting of eyeball-high pogo hops. If there was one upside to Ella's accident, it was this: her remaining hind leg had gotten as strong as a bull's.

A dancing bull's. Ella hooked her forepaws on my arm and tickled my cheek with her nose. "Down," I said, but I was already laughing.

Momma turned from Ella to shield our shopping bags, but she was smiling, too. "Take her out for a potty," she said. "I'll handle the groceries."

I didn't have to be told twice! I clipped on Ella's leash, looped it around my forearm and wrist, and led her downstairs to the back grass. I refuse to call it a backyard—the Jenkinses have a backyard. We just have back grass, because Ella can literally jump from one end of it to the other.

Which she did quite joyfully as soon as we got out there. Watching my little mutt hop across our tiny patch of green, I thought about Ricky's massive yard. I remembered all of the fun times Ella'd had there, sprinting free like a racing dog, her ears flapping like sails. A new thought entered my mind.

Ella had all sorts of different dog breeds in her background. What if one of Ella's parents or grandparents was a mean dog? Would that make her a little bit mean, too? There were too many questions—I needed to talk to a dog expert. Luckily, I had one on speed dial.

"Vanderstam Veterinary, how can I help you?" Miss Simon at our vet's office always answers the phone the exact same way. Just hearing her greeting made me relax a little. I eased my death grip on the cordless phone and reclined against my bedroom wall.

"Hi, Miss Simon," I said.

"Well, hello, Latasha!" She knew my voice because I always call her when Ella gets into mischief—in other words, pretty often. "Congratulations! You're our first call of the week."

I thought I might be. It was Monday at exactly 9:05 in the morning. I would have called right at nine, when the vet's office opens, but I'd waited until Momma got in the shower so that I could talk in private.

"I need a little help," I explained. Actually, I

needed more than a little. I was glad that Momma likes her showers extra-long on Mondays, so I'd have enough time to ask all of my questions. I could hear the water running and Momma was doing a cross between humming and singing behind the closed door.

"Uh-oh, what did Ella eat this time?" asked Miss Simon, her voice knowing and friendly.

"It's not what she ate," I said. "It's what she almost ate."

"Okay…what did Ella *almost* eat?"

"It's pretty bad," I said, my nerves tensing up. I knew that she wouldn't overreact like Momma or Mrs. Okocho might, but Miss Simon liked Ella a lot. I didn't want her to think less of my pup.

"It's probably not the worst," she replied.

I guessed that was true. My eyes ticked from left to right as I considered the best way to tell Miss Simon what Ella had done. "Well…"

Have you ever tried to pour a little milk into your cereal from a big gallon jug? If the jug is too full, it can slip out of your hands and spill all over the place. That's exactly what it was like once I started talking. I flooded the phone with every detail of Ella's afternoon—even the stuff that didn't matter, like how Darla Robinson gets on my nerves with her perfect little braids and her barrettes that match her shoes, and how Ricky's family makes me sad sometimes for no reason at all.

"And I hurried her home, and on Saturday I cried, and on Sunday I felt sorry for us both, and now it's Monday and I want to make Ella better, so I'm calling you." I sucked in a breath. I felt like Ella probably does after a bout of the zoomies. She was watching me curiously from the throw rug on my bedroom floor. "Sorry," I added.

"Don't worry about it," Miss Simon told me.

"So, what I want to know is…" I listened for the sound of running water, to make sure Momma wouldn't overhear. "Do you think Ella is part mean-dog?"

"Ella's a little sweetheart," Miss Simon replied.

"She didn't look like it on Saturday," I said doubtfully.

"Well, did she show her teeth or growl at you?"

"No."

"Did she do that to any other people?"

"No," I repeated, wondering where Miss Simon was headed.

"That's good," she said. "It would be a problem if she was aggressive—do you know what *aggressive* means?"

I'd known that word since the first week I had my pocket dictionary. "It describes someone who is forceful or attacking," I answered.

"I thought you might," Miss Simon said. "Anyway, it would be a real problem if Ella was aggressive toward people, but she didn't pick a fight with a person. She picked a fight with another dog. Some breeds aren't good with other dogs. Others just have a strong prey drive."

I peered at Ella on the floor. "What the heck would a dog have to pray about?"

Miss Simon chuckled. "Not *pray* with an 'a.' *Prey* with an 'e.'"

"Like a bird of prey?" I asked. I'd learned about hunter birds on a class trip to the Pittsburgh Zoo last spring.

"That's right," Miss Simon replied. "In dogs, prey drive shows up in different ways. It makes a sheep dog want to round up sheep. It makes some dogs want to follow a scent, and others want to chase a ball."

"Or a turkey," I said, looking at Ella. Believe it or not, that was how she had gotten away from me last fall. We were on a walk together when we'd spotted a wild turkey, right in the middle of the city! I was so surprised that I let my guard down—and Ella was so interested that she ripped free from my grip and chased after it.

"Prey drive in action," Miss Simon agreed. "It can make certain breeds of dogs very sensitive around other dogs."

"How can I figure out if Ella's got one of those breeds in her?" I asked.

"There are blood tests that'll tell you all about a dog's breeding," Miss Simon said. A smile crept across my face. I could find out Ella's whole history, all with a simple test! "But they're not exactly cheap," she added.

My smile melted into a smirk. Momma wouldn't like *not exactly cheap*. We were still on a payment plan from Ella's leg surgery. That's why Momma was taking extra Saturday shifts.

Miss Simon must have sensed my disappointment through the phone. "But don't worry about the test," she said. "It won't solve your problem. There's really only one way to make Ella calm around other dogs."

The shower turned off—I only had another minute to talk. "I'll try anything," I whispered.

"You have to work on her socialization," Miss Simon said.

Socialization. I pictured each syllable in my head—that helps me sometimes when I meet a new word. "Is that like Ella's social skills?" I asked.

"Bingo," Miss Simon replied. "Social skills take training. For dogs and people, really. You should slowly introduce Ella to your friend's dog. Take them for a walk together—work your way up to playtime. The more you get Ella used to this new dog, the less sensitive she'll be. Who knows? Maybe they'll really get along!"

I loved the idea of Ella having a new dog-friend. But what if it was too late? What if Ricky's parents didn't want to give Ella another chance? Or, even worse, what if Ricky didn't? What if Ella's outburst had given him a good hard shake and his Magic 8 Ball mind had decided *I don't want to be friends*?

"Did you hear me?" asked Miss Simon.

I shook the questions out of my head. "What?"

"I said I need you to promise me—when you start socializing the dogs, make sure you have adults around. Deal?"

The bathroom door opened and Momma stepped out. "Deal," I said. I thanked Miss Simon and clicked off the call.

"Who was on the phone?" asked Momma as she dried her ears with a towel.

A wrong number, a telemarketer, a prank caller— "Miss Simon," I admitted.

Momma only raised an eyebrow. "Uh-oh, what'd Ella eat this time?"

I really wanted to take Miss Simon's advice. I wanted Ella to become best friends with that Great Dane. But I was nervous to even talk to the Dane's owner.

So I kept finding excuses to stay in the house until I felt ready to face Ricky. Most of those excuses involved playing games with Ella and reading picture books to her. But since Momma was away at work during the week, the rest involved Mrs. Okocho.

We watched two hours of cartoons together one day, and the next day she taught me how to sew a button back onto one of her cardigans. "Someday," she said, "I will teach you to play cards."

On one clear, not-too-hot afternoon, Mrs. Okocho suggested that I pick the weeds in her garden for her. "I would do so myself, but my knees," she said, giving each one a gentle tap. "They are conspiring against me." I would have been fine with helping—especially because Mrs. Okocho offered to pay me a dime for every weed I picked—but if Ricky came outside to shoot hoops in his driveway or walk his dog or something, he'd surely stop over and I'd have to face him whether I wanted to or not.

Instead, we ended up having "drawing class." Mrs. Okocho explained that she would bring out an object and we would draw it in pencil exactly as we saw it. I just hoped it would be less boring than it sounded. "This I studied some years ago, at the community college," she told me. "We drew a bowl of fruits. But all I have are yams. I hope you do not mind."

She gulped down the bottom of her coffee mug and went to the kitchen to fetch them. This did not sound promising. Not only are yams deadly dull, but they're gross. They're slimy and way too sweet and they make a slurping, *floop*-y sound when you dump the chunks out of the can. I don't even like their pale orange color—they're like carrots that caught the flu.

But when Mrs. Okocho returned, she didn't have the canned yams I was picturing. She carried a mixing bowl that held a heap of what looked like oversized potatoes covered in tree bark.

"Feast your eyes on these beauties!" Mrs. Okocho said. She cautiously lowered the bowl to the table. I was amazed she'd made it without the pile spilling to the floor.

"So that's what a yam looks like?" I guessed I'd never seen a whole one before.

Mrs. Okocho looked at me as if I'd asked for a

ride to Mars. "Are you for real?"

My cheeks got hot. "Well," I sputtered, "why on Earth do you have so many of them?"

"Because they taste heavenly," she replied, like I should have been born knowing the answer. "Also, I can only find the true African yams some of the time. I must keep a reserve." Her eyes flashed with inspiration. "Latasha, you must try one!"

"I'm…not hungry," I said uneasily.

"Oh, but you must!" she exclaimed. "There are so many ways to prepare a yam. Boiled yams, stewed yams, fried yams in pepper sauce…or I could make for you my homemade sweet purple yam jam!"

Mrs. Okocho had grown on me over the last year, but I was pretty sure that her food ideas never would. "You go ahead and have a snack," I said, slipping out of my chair. "I'll check on Ella."

"Suit yourself," she said, already scanning the bowl for the perfect yam—if there is such a thing. "But soon, the aroma of my sweet purple yam jam will fill this house and your mouth will begin to water."

More like my eyes'll start to water, I thought. I could just imagine the sickeningly sweet smell of the cooking yams drifting up through our floor vents. There was only one place I could go to escape it:

outside. And if I wanted to go outside, I knew what I'd have to do.

I trudged across the street toward Ricky's. When I reached the door, I wasn't sure whether to knock or ring the bell. The strangest noises can make dogs go wild—for example, Ella's terrified of our oven timer and also of the sound Momma's cell phone makes when it gets low on battery. I didn't want to make Ricky any more upset with me by getting his puppy all riled up. To be honest, I really wanted to run back home and hide in Mrs. Okocho's flowerbed.

Knock, ring, or run? I wondered. In the end, it didn't matter. Just as I settled on knocking, the front door flew open and Ricky charged smack into me. "Oof!" I stumbled backward and fell in the grass on my rear end.

"Hey, perfect timing!" Ricky said, breaking into a grin. He was holding an envelope in one hand. He offered his free one to help me up.

I instantly forgot about my nervousness and slapped his hand away. "Why don't you watch where you're going?" I said, pushing myself to my feet.

"Says the girl who just hangs out on other people's

doorsteps," he replied. "This is for you."

He handed me his envelope. Written on the front in very fancy, very neat cursive were the words *Thank You*. "Or I guess I should say it's for *Ella*," he told me. "After all, she wrote that book for me, right?"

I had to think for a moment before I remembered that I'd given Ella author credit on Ricky's birthday present. "She's a pretty great writer, huh?" I asked.

Ricky smiled widely. "The best writer I know."

I put the thank you note in my back pocket. I didn't want to open it until I could share it with my pup. "So…" I began, hooking my thumbs into my belt loops. "You don't hate us? For wrecking your party?"

"I was ticked about the cake at first," Ricky admitted. "But Dad said that dogs tussle sometimes. We'll work it out."

Part of me felt relieved that Ricky was being so nice. But another part was annoyed that I'd spent so much time worrying over nothing. "Why didn't you come by and say something sooner?" I demanded.

"I've been super busy," Ricky replied. "You know, with Ham."

Yams, ham—what was it with food today?

Ricky's eyebrows went up. "Oh, man," he cried, "you haven't met Ham!" He yanked his front door open and hurried in. I guessed that was my cue to follow him.

I closed the door and slipped off my shoes. "I'm back!" Ricky shouted. "Latasha's with me!"

Mrs. Jenkins poked her head into the hallway from the dining room. "Hi, Latasha," she said, and then she ducked out of sight.

Ricky cupped his hands to call up the stairs. "Ham!" he exclaimed. "Ham, boy! C'mere!"

As Ricky whistled, I realized what was going on. "You named your Great Dane *Ham*?"

Ricky shook his head. "His name's Hamlet," he explained. "I wanted to name him Casey Hampton, since Great Danes get so big and all. But Dad said I ought to name him Hamlet." Ricky shrugged. "I figure, as long as there's 'Ham' in it. Ham! Come down, Ham!"

"Honey?" asked Mrs. Jenkins. She had returned to the hallway. "I don't think he's really learned his name yet. How about you go get him?"

Ricky did his trademark dramatic sigh. "You wait down here," he said to me. "This could take awhile. Lazy guy likes naps more than I do!" He bounded up the stairs.

Mrs. Jenkins gave me a head shake that said one word: *Boys*. "Well, back to work," she said, and she retreated into the dining room again.

I waited a few seconds, and when Ricky didn't return, I padded over to see what Mrs. Jenkins was up to.

I found her leaning over a large sheet of off-white poster board that was spread across the table. She was carefully drawing a line on the sheet with an odd-looking pen. Once Mrs. Jenkins had finished the line, I spoke. "I'm sorry about the trouble with Ella."

Mrs. Jenkins looked up and smiled warmly. "It's all right," she told me. "But thank you for the apology." She drew another line.

"What kind of pen is that?" I asked.

Mrs. Jenkins held the pen out for me to see. It had a feather at one end and a shiny, needle-sharp tip at the other. "It's a calligraphy pen," she explained. "*Calligraphy* means 'beautiful writing.'"

I would have to jot that down in my special vocabulary notebook when I got home: *calligraphy – a beautiful word that means beautiful writing*. Then I remembered the beautiful *Thank You* written on the envelope in my back pocket. I picked it out by a corner and held it up for Mrs. Jenkins to see. "Yours?" I asked.

"Well, the note on the inside is all Ricky," she said. "I did some envelopes to warm up for my little project here. I haven't used my pens in a while, so I was kind of rusty."

"I do arts and crafts sometimes with Mrs. Okocho," I ventured. Except that Mrs. Jenkins's project looked a lot more interesting than sketching a bunch of icky yams.

"Then maybe you'll appreciate this," she said. Ricky's mom moved her leather pen case aside and spun the large poster board for me with a grainy *whoosh*.

"It's for Mr. Jenkins's parents," she said. "It's their fiftieth anniversary this fall."

"Gosh," I said. I studied the poster board—which I realized when I touched its edge wasn't poster board at all, but some kind of cloth or canvas. At its top was a single line, with a single name written beside it in Mrs. Jenkins's fancy script: *Crafton Jacob Jenkins (1836 – 1874).* From the top line, three more lines branched out in a row, each with a name beside it. From those, more lines and names spread across a third row. Some lines died out, but most of them continued to blossom, getting more and more complicated.

"This is the complete Jenkins family tree," Mrs. Jenkins said, "starting with Ricky's great-great-great-great grandfather, Crafton. Mr. Jenkins gathered up all of the records, and I'm putting them on this nice vellum so we can get it framed. That's what you call this fancy paper—vellum."

"I bet they'll like that," I said quietly. I stared at the clusters of names, with their clean lines and beautiful labeling. It was so big, though, that my eyes couldn't hold it all at once. The longer I looked, the less the picture looked like a tree. It turned into a maze.

"I hope so," Mrs. Jenkins replied. "It took Ricky's dad forever to track it all down. Family histories can get kind of messy."

Something felt wrong inside me. That heart-underwater feeling was inching up again, but something else had come with it—something spicy, even angry—and it was all pushing against my ribs. I didn't understand what was making me so upset. It was just a dumb picture.

Except that it wasn't dumb. Not even a little.

"Latasha?" asked Mrs. Jenkins.

"I'm sorry, I just remembered something," I said, fumbling for any excuse. "I have to run home." And for the second time in two visits to Ricky's, that's exactly what I set out to do.

When I reached the door, Ricky came down the stairs with Hamlet walking slowly beside him. "Where are you going?" he said. "I just got him out of bed!"

"I'm sorry," I said, and I hurried out the door.

I sat in our apartment, my legs stretched on the couch, Ella curled at my feet. I was looking at the scribbles I'd made in my vocabulary notebook.

My notebook had started as a way to keep track of words I learned. But after Ella's accident, I'd started using it to keep track of my feelings, too. It really helped me on tough days, when my pup felt extra sore and I felt extra guilty.

I'd planned to write about Ricky's family tree, but when I opened the book, I realized that I didn't want to write. I wanted to draw.

I started to make a family tree of my own. I began mine in reverse, working back from me. I wrote my name at the bottom, *Latasha Esther Gandy (January 21, 2003 –)*, and a dotted line beside me pointed to *Ella Fitzgerald Gandy (April Fool)*. Above my name, I drew a big "T" shape. On the left of the "T" I wrote down Momma—or *Stephanie Gandy (February 13, 1982 –)*, to make it official. I went back along Momma's side to label her brother who lives in Las Vegas, and her parents, who I never got to meet because they both passed away while Momma was a teenager. I also filled in a few great-aunts and uncles from Momma's family down in Atlanta. "That's where the Gandys originally lived," I explained to my pup.

Then I went back to the "T" above my name so that I could start my dad's family on the right. I wrote my father's name: *Patrick Kidd.* After his name, I added a *?* That was where his birthdate would have gone if I'd known it.

That was all I had. And that hurt so bad that it made my face twitch.

"Why am I worried about where you came from?" I asked Ella, my voice breaking. "I don't even know where I came from."

Chapter Three

New Dog

This might sound bad to admit, but honestly, I don't much miss my father. I think about him sometimes—a lot, lately—but I don't miss him. You have to know somebody to miss him, and I know the look of Dad's handwriting better than I really know him. I've only met him a few times, but he sends me a funny birthday card every January and a manila envelope with money in it that matches my age. This year, he gave me $12.69—or nine one-dollar bills, nine quarters, and nine each of dimes, nickels, and pennies. That's how I know that my dad is not a bad person. Nobody who makes me smile just by the way he puts money in an envelope could be bad. But other than that, I know very little about him.

He works as a musician, but I don't know what instrument he plays. He lives in a place called Ambridge, which is forty-five minutes north of Pittsburgh—but usually he is traveling all over for different gigs. That's the word musicians use for their concerts. His looks are fuzzy to me. But he's very tall, and I could never forget his blazing red hair—redder than Ella's, even—which makes his skin seem even paler than it really is. Pale like a ghost.

"Wait a sec, wait a sec," Ricky interrupted, holding Ella at arm's length to escape her frantic licking. "Your dad's *white*?"

I glared at him. "And?"

"And nothing," he said quickly. "Just didn't know, that's all. You look like your mom."

I guessed it would be surprising—if my dad and I were walking down the street together, no one would assume we were related. And Momma's very pretty when she's not tired from work, so that could even be a compliment. But Ricky's voice felt like a punch in the stomach. "Okay," I replied. I sat unmoving on the porch.

It was the day after I'd fled Ricky's dining room. After Momma left for work, he'd stopped by to make plans for how we would introduce our dogs. We quickly decided that since tomorrow was Saturday, and Momma wasn't picking up any extra shifts for a change, we would have her and Mr. Jenkins bring the dogs out to the street. Then, with lots of encouragement (and even more treats), we'd try to get Ella and Hamlet to walk nicely next to each other.

I wasn't sure why I'd brought my dad up. Maybe I

wanted to try to explain why I'd run away yesterday. But I hadn't even gotten that far before Ricky had shut me up with, "Your dad's *white*?" Like that was all that mattered. Now I sat in stony silence, wishing I hadn't said anything—wishing my friend hadn't even come over.

Ella, on the other hand, couldn't have been happier to see Ricky. At the moment, she'd tangled herself in her leash with her wild pinwheeling, and Ricky's face and shirt were wet from her slobbery tongue. She was sniffing him all over, too, poking him in the side with her nose.

I was dead-set against smiling, no matter how cute Ella got. But then Ella's nose jabbed Ricky's ticklish spot and he let out a girly "Ooh-hooh!" I covered my mouth with my hand, pretending that my nose itched.

"What has gotten into her?" he sighed. "She's even crazier than usual."

I lowered my hand and cracked a sly smile. "It's probably because you stink like Ham."

"He doesn't stink," Ricky muttered. He shifted his weight. "I don't think he likes me."

"Impossible," I said without a pause.

"He doesn't like me like she does," he said, scratching Ella under the collar. "He doesn't even run to say hi when I come into the house. He just walks."

"Ham probably just has…a slower motor," I said. "Maybe if Ella gets used to him, she'll slow down a little, he'll speed up a little, and they'll both be normal."

Ricky smiled as he imagined our pair together. "We'll see tomorrow, huh?"

"How about two o'clock?" I suggested. I figured that would give Momma time to go to the Laundromat and handle whatever other Saturday chores we had lined up.

Ricky stood and said, "See you two at two!" He leaned in and rubbed behind Ella's ears, adding in a weird voice, "Won't I, girl!"

"Get out of here, goofy," I laughed.

"It's not Goofy, it's Scooby-Doo!" Ricky retorted. He cocked a thumb at my pup. "Ella got it."

Her tail was wagging so hard that it bent her body like a crescent moon. I got up to take her inside.

"Hey," Ricky called after me. "I'm sorry about— you know…"

"Thanks," I said, and I meant it.

"Why don't you just ask your mom to tell you about him?"

The thought of that sent a chill through me. "You know that saying," I replied, "if you can't say something nice, don't say anything at all?"

Ricky nodded.

I choked up on Ella's leash to bring her closer. "Momma never, ever says anything about my dad."

Our little Saturday dog-date almost didn't happen at all. That was because of Momma. She wasn't too busy or anything—it's just that when I asked her to help, she made me start at the beginning and explain precisely why we had to be so careful introducing the dogs.

Looking back, I probably shouldn't have gotten so detailed.

"Oh," she said, pressing a hand to her neck as I described the snarling and the charging. "Oh, that's embarrassing."

Honestly, I'd forgotten how much it might upset Momma to hear about it all for the first time. I'd gotten so used to the fact that the scuffle happened that it just felt like another story to me. By the time I reached the table-flipping and the flying presents and the cake-smashing, Momma'd had enough. "Latasha *Esther* Gandy," she said, her voice getting louder and higher, "why did you not tell me about this before?"

This is exactly why, I thought. I hate it when Momma uses my middle name like that. I'm not a fan of the name *Esther* even on a good day, but when Momma's mad, she spits it out like a curse word.

Rather than bring that up, though, I told her, "I wanted to protect Ella." The pup watched us from my bedroom's doorway, belly flat on the floor. "I didn't want her to get punished."

"And I guess you forgot our deal about keeping secrets?" Momma scolded. "This is a—"

"No-secrets family," I said along with her. "I'm sorry."

She looked at me, the fire in her eyes slowly cooling. "I hope you apologized to the Jenkinses," she told me.

"I did," I said, nodding sharply. "Mrs. Jenkins said everything was okay."

Momma pursed her lips at Ella. "And you," she said, shaking her head. The pup seemed to sink even farther into the carpet.

"She didn't mean to start trouble," I insisted.

Momma tucked her chin and shot a look at me from under her brow. As soon as the spotlight was off of her, Ella scrambled into my room, out of sight. I could hear her paws scratching the carpet as she shoved herself under my bed.

"See how bad she feels?" I said. "She messed up, Momma, and she knows it. I just want to give her another chance."

Momma didn't respond. I crossed over to her and gripped her hand. "Doesn't everybody deserve a second chance?" I asked.

"Everybody?" Momma squeezed my hand back. She sighed. "They want to meet at two, you said?"

At two o'clock exactly, the whole Gandy family stepped out onto the porch. I held a baggie of Teddy Snacks and Momma clutched Ella's leash, double-wrapped around her hand.

"Sit," Momma said as Ella danced in the hot, dry air.

But before Ella could even decide whether to obey, Ricky's front door opened and he stepped out by himself. When he waved, Ella wagged so hard she nearly made herself hover.

"Ouch!" Momma said as Ella's happy tail snapped against her calves. "Watch that thing!"

"It hurts even worse in the winter," I said, grinning.

"They'll be out in a minute," Ricky yelled from his front steps. "Ham's being fussy."

Momma glanced at me, then down at Ella, who was struggling so hard to go to Ricky that it was making her cough. "Let's get to it," she said doubtfully.

Ella's tags jangled as we slowly let her down the stairs. She dragged Momma straight toward Ricky, not even stopping to sniff the gutter or the base of the tree out front.

"Hi, Miss Gandy," Ricky said.

"Hot enough for you?" Momma replied, wiping her forehead with the back of her free hand. It always feels about fifteen degrees hotter than it is when you've got to hold onto Ella.

Ricky knelt to scratch behind Ella's ears. "So where are we doing this?" he asked me.

"Sidewalk," I replied. "No yards. The sidewalk is like neutral ground."

Ricky pointed a finger in agreement. "Got your treats?" he asked.

I held up the baggie of Teddy Snacks and shook it. Ella instantly spun back and sat for me.

"Very good!" Momma exclaimed.

"This won't be so hard," I replied, feeding Ella a crunchy treat.

But then, Ricky's front door opened once again. Mrs. Jenkins led the way out, followed by Mr. Jenkins—followed by Hamlet, who plodded behind them.

In an instant, Ella's fur jutted up and she was tugging and barking meanly. No, she sounded worse than mean—she sounded ferocious. "Girl, no!" Momma said sternly, wrapping the leash another time around her wrist. She looked at Ricky's parents. Mr. Jenkins was holding Hamlet back, because the Great Dane was growling now himself. "I am so sorry about her," Momma said.

I was so embarrassed by Ella's behavior that it made the back of my neck tingle. But I refused to let it scare me off. Not this time. I pushed my brain to come up with a solution—anything to help Ella calm down. After a few seconds, two words entered my mind: *New Dog.*

"How about we take her for a lap around the block?" I suggested to everyone. "She can cool off and we'll start over."

"Good idea," Mr. Jenkins said.

I took Momma's arm and led her and Ella off. Once we'd passed a few houses, Ella stopped straining and walked along with us. I fed her three Teddy Snacks as we moved down the block. "Good girl!" I said.

"Should you really be rewarding her?" Momma asked me.

It was one of those questions that isn't really a question at all, but I answered anyway. "I have a plan."

"I just don't think Ella's ready to make a friend," Momma said.

Almost like she understood, Ella stopped so short that Momma nearly crashed into her. The pup shook herself until her spiky fur settled, and then she darted onward, all floppy tongue and wagging tail.

"Look at her," I said as we marched along. "She's already forgotten about what happened. It's like New Dog at home."

"New Dog, huh?" Momma replied.

New Dog is the name we have for this odd thing Ella does at dinner. Every night while we eat, Ella sits and waits next to one of us for a scrap. Except she doesn't really wait at first—she cries, she begs, she even demands by putting her paw on someone's knee. None of that works on us, of course. She only gets her treat once she stops begging and sits patiently.

On most nights, one bit of pork chop gristle or a single piece of broccoli is enough to satisfy her. But on some nights, one treat is simply not enough. That's where New Dog comes in.

When Ella wants another treat, she doesn't immediately start begging again. Instead, she gets up, trots around the whole table, then sits back down in her exact original spot. As if that would somehow convince us that she's not the little red cutie we just treated—that must've been some *other* dog. So that's what I say when Ella returns: "Oh, look, Momma! It's a new dog!"

The crazy thing, though, is this: when she comes back around, Ella really does behave like a new dog. And each New Dog version of her is better behaved than the last. A round-two New Dog doesn't demand a treat with her paw—she'll only whimper. The round-three version won't even cry—she'll just sit. A round-four doesn't sit—she lies down without even being asked.

I guessed that we'd need Ella to be at least a round-seven-or-eight New Dog before she could walk nicely with Hamlet.

We reached the corner at Coral Street and crossed back to our side of the road. "We'll go a few houses past Ricky's," I said, "then cross back over and try again."

"You're the boss," Momma replied. I sure liked the sound of that!

We passed the Jenkinses, Graham Street dividing us. I fed Ella a whole fistful of treats to keep her attention off Hamlet, who was lazing at Ricky's feet. Then we looped back around for a second try.

"New dog!" I told Ella.

Same old dog. We got about one house away from the Jenkins family before the fur shot up and the barking began. Ella growled and cried as she tried to tug Momma over toward Ham, but Momma and Mr. Jenkins kept them apart pretty easily this time.

"One more try?" I asked as we hustled our noisy pup past.

Mr. and Mrs. Jenkins both nodded kindly.

Ricky followed us for a few steps. "You're not fooling anyone with that tough girl act," he called out. "Everybody knows you're just a big softie."

I decided he meant Ella. My girl shook herself calm and I petted her from neck to tail. "You're doing so well!" I told her. "You shook that prey drive right out!"

I looked up at Momma. "We need to both tell her how great she's doing," I said. "If we make her feel good about herself, she'll try even harder next time."

Momma gave me an amused smirk. "Oh, yeah?" she asked. "Where'd you pick up that idea?"

I was stunned that she had to ask. "From you!"

Momma finished our lap around the block with one hand grasping Ella's leash and the other on my shoulder.

On the third pass, Ella didn't lunge at Hamlet— she just growled and cried and yipped. "That was awesome, Ella!" Momma said.

"You're doing better every time," I added, feeding her more Teddy Snacks.

It was true. By the fifth round of New Dog, Ella had stopped growling. And in the seventh round…

The two dogs walked side by side for three whole houses.

"You're doing it!" Ricky exclaimed, clapping his hands.

"You'll get them riled up again," I warned.

But inside, I felt the same as he did. I was so proud of Ella that I could have shouted the news from the top of Mount Washington.

"What do you think?" Momma asked me after we'd circled around once more.

Ella and Hamlet were sitting just a couple of feet apart, both panting heavily. "I think that's enough for today," I replied, beaming.

"Sounds right to me," Mr. Jenkins agreed. "I think these pups are wiped out."

Mrs. Jenkins poked him with her elbow. "Them or you?"

"Don't worry, I'm still grilling tonight," he said, hooking an arm around his wife's waist.

"Hamburgers for Ham!" Ricky promised his dog.

I turned away from the Jenkinses and focused on giving Ella my last few Teddy crumbs.

"But if you two are around tomorrow," Mr. Jenkins told Momma, "we can train some more."

I bounced back up to my feet.

"You're the best, Dad!" Ricky said.

"Really? Are you sure?" asked Momma.

I thought about that gift horse she'd once told me about and nodded for encouragement.

Mr. Jenkins smiled at me. "Definitely."

"Perfect!" Mrs. Jenkins said. "Latasha, Ricky— let's get a photo. Puppies and their trainers."

After learning the Jenkinses' dinner plans, Momma and I were both in the mood to run the grill ourselves. The only trouble is that we don't own a grill, or even have a good space to use one anyway. So instead, we improvised our own barbecue.

Juices sizzled in the frying pan as Momma turned our hot dogs with metal tongs. "You did a great job with her today," she said, glancing back at me from the stove.

I was seated at the kitchen table, one bare foot resting on Momma's chair, the other on the floor. In front of that foot, for the first time since Ricky's party, Ella lay totally exhausted on her side. Our training session had gone better than I could have hoped— but the other thing I had on my mind had started to slink back in. I needed to talk to Momma about it, but what if it ruined our perfect night?

"Grab the buns," Momma instructed.

I went to the bread drawer at the counter and fetched the hot dog buns. "Can I toast them?"

"*May* I," replied Momma. Then she winked. "And it wouldn't be a barbecue without toasted buns."

I pulled a handful of buns from the plastic bag and opened them flat. Then I popped a pair into the toaster. I returned to my chair and settled down again in front of Ella.

Momma hummed as she turned the hot dogs once more.

We're a no-secrets family, I reminded myself. That meant I owed it to Momma to tell her what I was thinking.

"So, Momma…" I began, trying to sound as casual as can be. "What do you think of Mr. Jenkins?"

She shrugged without turning. "He's nice."

"I think he's a really good dad," I replied.

Momma threw a smile back toward me. "I'll bet he is."

The toaster went off and our browned bun-tops popped into view. I tucked my toes under Ella's warm belly. "Ricky's…pretty lucky to have him around."

Momma's back stiffened. She turned off the stove

burner and faced me.

"Momma…" I said, pausing to wish the shakiness away. "Do you think Dad ever wonders about me?"

She stepped toward me slowly, as if the lights had gone out and she didn't want to trip. "Are you thinking about him?" she asked.

There was no more dancing around it. "I want to call him," I replied. "I want to talk to him."

Momma sat in the chair beside mine and didn't say a word.

"Are you mad at me?" I asked.

"Not at all," she said firmly. "Why would I be mad?"

My stomach tightened like a pulled rubber band. "Because you hate him."

Momma let out a low sigh. "I don't hate your father, sweetie."

"Then why don't you want me to know him?" I demanded.

Under the fluorescent kitchen light, Momma's eyes looked almost like they were glowing. Quietly she replied, "It's not that."

The rubber band in my belly snapped and I felt myself sinking into the chair. "He doesn't want to know me."

"It's not that, either," Momma told me. "Your

father is a…" She flexed her hands like she wished to grab the words. "Your father made a choice. Years and years ago. And that choice was to not be part of this family."

Something dripped onto my hand and I realized that I was crying. Before I could even sniffle, Momma reached over and wiped my cheeks with her thumb. Her palm was still warm from handling the frying pan. Once the tears stopped, Momma went on.

"I don't hate your father," she repeated. "I'm not even mad at him anymore. I feel sad for him sometimes, because he is missing out on something wonderful."

She pressed her pointer finger gently to the tip of my nose. It made my whole body relax. Ella must have felt it, too, because from below the table I heard a loud, heavy huff of breath. I peeked at her and tickled her ribs with my toes.

"Honey," Momma said, "what brought all this on?"

"I'm tired of being jealous of Ricky," I said. "Best friends shouldn't be jealous of each other."

"People get jealous sometimes," Momma replied. "It doesn't make you a bad friend."

I nodded, but I wasn't sure I believed her.

"Can I try calling Dad?" I asked. "I think it would help."

Momma touched her chin as she thought. Her mouth opened to speak, but the wrinkles in her brow had already told me everything.

"Momma, please?" I interrupted. "If he says, 'No, I don't want to talk,' fine. But…don't I deserve a chance?"

Momma hung her head and smiled to herself.

I couldn't tell what kind of smile it was. It made me nervous—had I pushed too hard? "What?" I asked.

"You've definitely got one part of him," she said. Her hand fell on top of mine. "You're both very hard to say 'no' to."

My heart began to thump like a drum. "Does that mean…?"

Momma rose from her chair and, for a moment, she looked twice her age. She moved like Mrs. Okocho does after she's been in her rocking chair for too long.

"I'll call him tonight," she told me. "I'll try to set something up."

I almost had to check the floor to make sure I hadn't started floating. Momma looked toward our dinner at the counter and said, "Our hot dogs turned into cold dogs."

Chapter Four

Common Grounds

The next weekend, Momma and I came home from our first round of back-to-school clothes shopping to find the phone ringing. Ella couldn't decide which excited her more—our return or the ringing phone—so the moment we entered, she began to spring to and fro across the kitchen.

"Settle down, wild thing!" Momma said, holding our Goodwill bags high out of reach. "Honey, grab that, would you?"

I swung a bag that held my light green first-day-of-school jumper onto the table, and then swiped the phone off the wall mount.

"Gandy residence!"

"Uh-oh," the voice on the line said. "I think I might have the wrong number. I'm trying to reach my little girl, Latasha…but you sound *way* too grown up to be her."

My eyes became platters. "Daddy!"

"Hey there, jelly bean," he said. And just like that, Dad was back in my life.

Except it wasn't really just like that. It had been a whole week and a day since Momma promised to get me in touch. A week and a day, and a turn of the calendar from July to August. A week and a day, and a calendar turn, and three more Ella and Hamlet play dates—and one call between Momma and Dad that I couldn't help but overhear.

"No email," I'd heard Momma say. "An honest-to-goodness phone call."

"Oh," she'd snapped, "I'm sure you've got *plenty*

going on."

"I ask you for very little, Patrick."

I hadn't been trying to listen in. It's just that when Momma gets cross, her voice cuts through doors, walls, and even pillows.

But none of that mattered now—my dad had finally called, and he'd called just for me.

"You still there, kid?" he asked.

"I'm here, I'm here," I said quickly. I cupped my hand over the receiver. "Momma, may I take the phone to my room?"

Momma gave me a nod. "But leave your door open for me," she added.

I trotted off to my room. Ella stayed behind to bat at Momma's bags and beg for treats.

"Sorry about the noise," I told my dad as I settled onto my bed.

"No worries," he replied. "Sorry it took me a little while to call."

"It's okay, Daddy."

"So, my girl," he began. "What's the latest news in the world of Latasha?"

I thought for a few long seconds. Dad's question was a totally normal way to start a conversation, but it felt life-and-death important to answer it just right.

Out in the living room, Momma walked toward

her bedroom with some of our shopping bags, Ella sniffing behind her. Momma slowed down to glance at me as they passed.

"Momma and I just did back-to-school shopping," I said eagerly. That definitely fit under new, if not exactly exciting.

"Ugh," Dad replied. "I remember those days with my mum…and I do *not* miss them."

"What do you mean?" I asked. I loved shopping for new school outfits. And I was extra excited to start fourth grade at the end of the month. I couldn't wait to meet my new teachers and wrap my books in clean brown paper that I could write my name and draw little designs on—and most of all, I looked forward to the first meeting of Talent Pool with Mr. Harvey.

"I always hated school," Dad said. "Band was okay…but everything else? Gag me with a spoon."

"Oh." It was like a cloud of disappointment had settled down around my head. I almost didn't add the next part. "I kind of really like school."

"Well," Dad replied, pausing, "that's probably better."

More seconds that felt like minutes passed by. I saw Ella leave Momma's room and walk a lap around the couch.

"So aside from going out and, you know…buying

new pencils and whatnot," Dad said. "What else have you got going on?"

"I've been training my dog a lot," I said. I snapped my fingers to get Ella's attention. I hoped that she would come and make a warm little nest against my side.

"That's hard work, huh?" he replied.

Instead, the pup looked at me and then walked off to the kitchen. "The hardest," I sighed.

"Sounds like it," Dad said with a laugh.

"Did you ever have a dog growing up?"

"No way," he said. "I'm definitely not patient enough for a puppy. They just…*need* so much, you know?"

"…Oh." I wished I could have a do-over with this whole phone call, one that went more like the great calls I'd imagined all week.

"I did have a guinea pig once," Dad added hastily.

"Really?" I asked. "What was its name?"

"It was silly," he replied.

That sounded promising. "Come on, what was it?"

"Thelonious," he replied.

"What the heck kind of name is that?" I blurted it out before I could think of a nicer way to ask.

"Like I said!" Dad replied, laughing. "I named

him after this piano player I really liked. A jazz guy."

My face lit up. Finally—this was the sort of thing I'd been hoping to learn! "That's awesome," I said. "And it's kind of funny, too—"

"—Yeah," Dad cut in, "but I fed him cauliflower one night and he died."

I sighed so hard it flushed the air out of the room.

"It was pretty horrible," Dad said. "And gross, too."

I was totally out of words.

"Hey, kid…" Dad said. He chuckled, which actually made me really angry. "This whole…'us talking on the phone' thing?"

"It's okay, Dad," I murmured, clutching the edge of my mattress. I felt foolish for pushing to have this call—I just wanted to drop it. "If you have something you've got to do—"

"—No, it's not that," Dad replied.

I heard the crinkly slap of a plastic bag hitting the kitchen floor. *Great*, I thought bitterly. *Now Ella's eating my new dress.*

"It's just…" Dad went on. "It's a little awkward."

"Hang on," I grumbled. I hopped off the bed and marched toward the kitchen. I heard more thrashing of my Goodwill bag—I could already imagine my chewed-up, slobbery dress.

"I don't know how this stuff is supposed to work," Dad said. "You know?"

But when I reached the doorway, I didn't find a chewed-up dress. It hadn't even left the bag. Instead, Ella had somehow managed to knock the bag off the table and get its handles caught around her hind leg. She was whipping the bag (and my dress) from side to side against herself, trying to get free.

"Ella!" I laughed. I shielded myself from her frenzied tail and freed her leg from the bag. I petted Ella's neck and her wiggling slowed. "Oh, Ella Fitzgerald Gandy," I told her, "what am I going to do with you?"

"Everything all right?" I remembered that the phone was still clamped between my ear and shoulder.

"Yeah, it's just Ella, being her crazy self," I said. I stroked Ella's ears with my free hand and gave them each the gentlest little pull, like she likes.

"Wait, your dog's name is Ella Fitzgerald?" asked Dad. "Like the singer?"

"Yeah. Mom loves her."

"I know," Dad replied. "It was her idea, then?"

"No," I said, "it was mine."

"And it was your idea," he echoed, as if the words tasted like dessert. "That is…incredibly cool.

Actually, that might be the best dog name I've ever heard."

"Definitely beats Hamlet," I agreed.

"…Sure," Dad replied. "Hey, listen. I have a proposition for you. You want to hear it?"

I had to smile—I love when adults use big words around me and just assume I'll know what they mean. "What's your offer?" I asked.

"The past couple months," Dad said, "I've been sitting in here and there with this jazz band in the city. I don't know when they'll need me next, but when they do…I'd love to come in early and take you out for a coffee. What do you say?"

If I wanted our coffee date to go well, I needed to prepare. As far as I could figure, there were two things I needed to do to be ready.

First, I had to come up with some conversation starters. I thought it might take a while since it was so hard for me to do over the phone. But actually, it was easy. I just got my notebook, opened to a clean page in the back, and listed things I wanted to know. I stuck to simple questions—facts I really did want to learn, but nothing that would be awkward. I asked about little things, the kinds of details that I would want to know if I were to write a story about my dad. Like: *What's your favorite city to visit?* And: *When did you start playing your instrument?* Which led to something even more basic: *What actually is your instrument?* I'd wanted to ask on the phone, but when I got nervous I completely forgot.

I finished my list less than an hour after I'd started it. But the second thing I had to do for our coffee date wasn't so simple—I had to learn how to like coffee!

Momma only drinks tea at home, so I'd never had a chance to try coffee. To be honest, I'd never been interested before. But I didn't want to embarrass myself, like the time I tried grapefruit juice at Ricky's last winter and spat it all over the kitchen counter. Who knew that a drink with such a pretty pink color could end up tasting so nasty?

After Momma left for work on Monday, I decided to have coffee practice. I knew just the person to help me.

"Welcome, sit!" Mrs. Okocho led me to a chair at her huge dining room table. "You are timed perfectly. I am just about to fix a fresh pot." Mrs. Okocho is the biggest coffee drinker I know, even more than my teachers at school. It's her favorite drink, and she'll have it at any time of day—even an hour before bed, which makes absolutely no sense.

Now that I think about it, the fact that Mrs. Okocho loves coffee so much might be the reason I never cared to try it.

As I waited for the coffee to brew, I felt myself starting to sweat. I was a bit nervous, but mostly it was because Mrs. Okocho had all of her windows closed. The August heat had turned the dining room into a tropical jungle, and the potted plants that decorated the room didn't help that image.

Mrs. Okocho peeped around the doorframe. "You are sure that you would like a coffee?" she asked. "The flavor is very strong."

"Oh, I know," I bluffed.

"I can make cocoa with the cute little marshmallows," Mrs. Okocho offered. "Or by the look of you…perhaps a nice cool iced tea?"

Iced tea actually sounded perfect—but I was on a mission. "Thanks, Mrs. O," I replied, "but I could really go for a fresh cup of coffee. The hotter, the better."

"Ha-ha!" she cackled. "That is what I say as well!" She returned to the kitchen.

No kidding, I thought, dabbing at my neck with a napkin from the table holder.

Mrs. Okocho carried in a small bowl of sugar

cubes. "It is brewing," she said. "You *did* ask first your mama about this, yes?"

That was the one thing I hadn't done. I hadn't even mentioned that Dad wanted to take me for coffee— only that he wanted to visit me. I wasn't trying to break our no-secrets rule, exactly. It's just that I only got that far before a look crossed Momma's face. The look said *I'll believe it when I see it*. It made me not want to tell her anything else.

"It'll be fine," I said.

That seemed to satisfy Mrs. Okocho, because she continued fetching items from the kitchen. By the time our coffee was ready, she'd brought out three kinds of artificial sweeteners, a shaker of cinnamon, and two small ceramic jugs—one with cream, one with skim milk. I'd had no idea that coffee was so complicated!

Finally, Mrs. Okocho shuffled in with a pair of steaming mugs. "Here we are!" she announced. She set my cup in front of me and I let the steam waft up my nose. The smell was sharp, but not exactly bad.

Mrs. Okocho sat down and told me, "Go ahead, child. Fix it up however you like!" I watched her shake some cinnamon into her mug, add about four cubes of sugar, and then stir in some cream.

I liked all the things Mrs. Okocho was adding

into her coffee—but at the same time, it *was* Mrs. Okocho adding them. She had very odd tastes when it came to most foods. What if nobody but her put cinnamon in their coffee and it made me look weird?

"Is there something missing?" asked Mrs. Okocho. "I have nutmeg if you would like."

I had no idea what nutmeg was, but I guessed that I would probably *not like*. I decided to keep things simple and normal. "Thanks," I replied, "but I like my coffee plain."

"You mean black," Mrs. Okocho replied. "That is the name for plain coffee."

"Right," I replied, glancing at my inky beverage. "That's what I meant to say."

"Let it cool some, first," she suggested.

Once my mug got a little less steamy, I lifted it and took a drink. The moment I swallowed, all the saliva dried up in my mouth. My eyes and my lips scrunched toward each other like they wanted to trade places.

"Latasha," Mrs. Okocho said, "are you all right?"

I nodded, sucking on the sides of my tongue to try to get some moisture back.

"Are you sure you do not want something else to drink?"

I couldn't believe that my father wanted to take

me out for this disgusting, awful stuff!

"It's fine," I replied, trying not to gag. But my next sip was even worse than the first. All I could taste was bitterness, a hundred times worse than grapefruit—like I'd bitten a Tylenol in two.

"That is enough, I think," Mrs. Okocho said as she moved my coffee cup to her side of the table. "I refuse to let you suffer."

I hung my head in defeat.

"Would you like some water?" she asked.

I shrugged and Mrs. Okocho left the room. So much for not embarrassing myself—I was just glad it had happened here and not in front of my dad.

Mrs. Okocho returned with a glass of cold water. I took a mouthful of it and swished the terrible taste away. "Better?" she asked.

"Thanks," I said. "I don't know how people drink this stuff."

Mrs. Okocho waved an arm at the many sugars and spices on the table. "Most often, with help," she said. "What inspired this little…experiment?"

I hesitated for a second. I didn't want to go through the details—I'd done that enough in my head lately. After thinking, I landed on an answer that was simple and true. "I just want to be cool."

Mrs. Okocho smiled at me. "You, my child, are

already the coolest."

I smiled back and took another gulp of water. I'd never noticed how delicious it was.

"Mrs. Okocho," I finally said, "if someone wants to meet for coffee…I don't *have* to actually order coffee, do I?"

That night after dinner, I sat on our couch to read a novel from the library. Ella curled up at my feet like usual.

Momma came in with two small bowls of ice cream. "You want a dessert break?" she asked. Before I could even turn, Ella sprang from her slumber and draped her head over the back of the couch to stare at Momma.

"Not you, silly," Momma told her.

"Do we have blueberries?" I asked, replacing my bookmark.

"I'll put some on top," Momma replied.

Ella stared after Momma as she returned to the kitchen. "Dessert," I said. Ella's head whipped toward mine, her ears perked and alert. "Dessert," I repeated, and her ears jumped and flopped in response. It amazed me to discover what words Ella could learn when she thought they were important.

Momma returned with our fruit-topped ice cream and sat with me. For a minute we enjoyed our desserts in silence—except for Ella, whose tail quietly thumped the couch cushion as she waited for leftovers.

Momma wiped the corner of her mouth. "Sorry I don't have any…coffee to go with it," she said.

I couldn't believe that Mrs. Okocho had blabbed! She must have caught Momma before she came upstairs. "You heard about that, huh?" I said.

"What's going on?" she asked.

There was no sense trying to be cute about it. I explained about Dad's visit, and how important it was to be ready. When I finished, Momma took a bite of ice cream and I waited. She finally replied, "So your father wants to take his nine-year-old out for coffee."

I stuck my spoon into my ice cream and swung my feet to the floor. "I'm full," I replied. "May I be excused?"

"Latasha," Momma said, "wait. I'm not trying to pick a fight."

"I'm going to have a mocha latte, anyway," I simpered, leaning back into the couch. "Mrs. Okocho taught me how to order one."

Momma gave me a small, sad smile. "Listen," she

said. "About your dad saying he'll visit?"

"He's going to," I replied. "It might be a while, like he said. But he will. He wasn't lying."

"I'm sure he wasn't," Momma said. "When he promised he'd take you out, he probably really meant it. But it's one thing to make a promise and another to keep it. I will not watch you waste the rest of your summer waiting for your father to turn one into the other."

"I'm not going to waste—"

"—Just make *me* a promise," Momma said, holding up her pointer finger.

I exhaled slowly. "What?"

"If your dad comes, great. I'll be happy that he did," she began. "But promise you won't plan your whole life around it. Play with Ricky, care for Ella…I don't know, be nine! Deal?"

As if she had to chime in, Ella settled her head across my lap and turned on her side. Her look took the fight right out of me. "Deal," I agreed.

"Good," Momma said, standing. "After all, you're a Gandy. And us Gandy girls? We don't sit around waiting for some man to call on us. No matter who he is."

Chapter Five
Talent Pool

Momma's talk about Dad had been frustrating—but the worst part was that she'd been completely and totally right. Weeks went by, all without a word from him. In fact, Momma and I seemed to hear from everyone *but* him.

A letter arrived from Miss Simon, reminding us to schedule a check-up for Ella. It had been almost a year since she'd lost her leg, and Dr. Vanderstam wanted to check the strength of the joints in her remaining three. We also got a packet from Mr. Harvey about his plans for this year's Talent Pool. Most of the packet was about this competition that the club entered every year. I'd heard of it around school before, but I didn't know much about it. It sounded neat, even if the name for the competition was a little silly.

"'The Innovation Conversation,'" Momma read to me. "'A problem-solving contest for exceptional students. Participating teams will work together to respond to open-ended challenges with creative thinking and style.'" Momma bumped her knee against mine. "Well, you've got plenty of both of those."

I looked away, blushing. "What do they mean about an open-ended challenge?"

Momma skimmed the flyer. "Ah!" she said. "After school starts, the folks who run this thing will give everyone three basic ideas to pick from. Then each team will use one of those ideas to inspire a performance project."

"Like a play?"

"Sure," Momma replied. "It says here: 'Team performances can include original videos, artwork, dance, skits, or live music.'"

After reading about the Innovation Conversation—or the I.C., which was a lot less silly-sounding—I was really excited to start Talent Pool. But I couldn't feel all the way excited. It was weird how quickly two little words like "live music" could bring Dad back to mind, along with the sad, lonely feeling that always followed. That never used to happen to me.

At least I had Ella, and Mrs. Okocho, and even goofball Ricky to keep me occupied. A week before school, on a day that had been especially rough, I spent a whole afternoon watching Ricky try to look cool while he showed off his latest toy—a drum pad.

Except he insisted, "It's not a toy."

Ricky's not-toy was a little mini snare drum, only the head was quiet when you hit it, like a pen slapping on a book cover. It was actually kind of cute.

"It's not cute, either," he said. "It's awesome. Right, Ham?"

Hamlet walked in a circle and flopped onto the carpet in Ricky's room.

"I thought your folks were getting you a drum set," I said.

"They will," he told me, absently clicking his drumsticks together. "This is just for practice. Maybe next year I can get the real thing."

I started to wonder if my dad had learned on a fake instrument when he was our age. But the next thing Ricky did pushed that thought away.

"Besides," he said, giving the drum pad a tap. "I can still rock out on this."

Watching Ricky rock out is like watching Ella try to catch her tail—it *almost* actually happens.

Before I knew it, the calendar turned again and it was September. "How do I look?" I asked Momma, smoothing out my dress. It was Tuesday morning and we were standing on the sidewalk outside Cedarville Elementary about ten minutes before the start of fourth grade.

"You look ready to take over the world," Momma replied. I glanced down at myself. I didn't know if anyone had conquered the world while wearing a bright green jumper—but I took the compliment anyway.

I slung my backpack high on my shoulder, careful not to whack any of the kids or adults who were milling past us. I watched all of the parents and guardians escort their kids to the steps. One mom gave each of her twin sons a rib-crushing hug. I saw Darla Washington from my grade laughing with her grandma, who winked at her and handed over a lunchbox with a picture of Ray Charles on the front. One dad lifted his kindergartner—I figured kindergarten because she'd worn a can't-miss-it pink ballet tutu—up above his head. That dad held her high above the crowd, like she was a prize he'd won and he wanted everyone to know.

I tried to imagine what that little girl felt like, but nothing came.

"Mrs. O will be waiting here at three," Momma said from behind me. She placed her hands on my shoulders and rubbed each one. "Knock 'em dead, sweetie."

The first day of fourth grade was the same as any other grade—except that Ricky wasn't in my homeroom. He was in the other fourth grade class, with Mr. Loch. I had Miss Prooper, who looked like a raisin but had a loud, mean, truck driver voice.

"Everything she says sounds like a threat," I told

Ricky when I met up with him at lunch. "Like, 'I know you'll do your best this year'…*or else*!"

"Her actual threats sound worse," said Ricky's friend Dante, who was also at our table. A bunch of us who'd had Mr. Harvey last year were sitting together.

"Dude," Ricky laughed. "How were you late to the first day of school?"

Dante puffed out his cheeks before he replied. "I don't know, man, I just was."

When the first bell rang, I'd thought that nobody I knew had ended up in my class, but then it turned out that Dante had. He just came in fifteen minutes late. When he entered, Miss Prooper went off on a rant about how disrespectful it was to be tardy, and how she would not tolerate it under any circumstance. She made Dante say who he was three whole times, and then she wrote his first name on the board—"So I'll *remember*."

"I know why she's so mean," Ricky said. "My friend Bud in fifth grade? He says the kids in his class called her Prooper-Scooper."

That was kind of gross, but it got a laugh out of me.

"I can't believe her parents named her Prooper," Dante said, shaking his head.

"That's her last name, doof," Ricky sneered.

"Nobody picks their last name."

"Whatever," was Dante's witty reply.

Ricky was wrong, though—some last names did get picked. In a way, my dad picked my last name. If he'd stayed, I might have wound up being Latasha Kidd. Latasha Esther Kidd, with my little mutt, Ella Fitzgerald Kidd. But these were the kinds of thoughts I'd been trying to stay away from. I needed to change the subject, and fast.

"So how's Mr. Loch?" I asked Ricky.

"He's no Mr. Harvey," he said with a sigh.

On the plus side, I didn't have to wait long to see our old teacher. That's because on Thursday, we had our first meeting of Gifted and Talented! Usually, our meetings would be held right after school, but this first meeting was for both the kids and our parents, so it took place in the evening. Even Momma was able to make it—except she hadn't had time to change all the way out of her work clothes. She'd switched to slacks but couldn't find a shirt to match, so she'd had to put a zip-up fleece on over her scrubs top.

"You can't tell, right?" asked Momma as we entered the school.

I looked her over. "Except for your ID," I said.

Momma saw that she'd forgotten to remove her bright pink nametag. "Very wise," she replied, and she unpinned the tag and stuffed it in her pocket.

We reached Mr. Harvey's classroom just in time, at one minute before eight o'clock. Half the seats were already filled with kids and parents. I saw Darla and her grandma, and a couple kids from my new class with their parents, but there were a lot of people I didn't recognize. One thing was for sure—adults look *weird* sitting at third-grader desks.

The front of the room, though, looked normal as ever—the "Classroom Star" chart hung next to the blackboard, announcing the students who had done good deeds that week; the little classroom library stood in the corner; Mr. Harvey's "Wanted: Read or Alive" recommended reading list was taped to the wall above it. And, of course, there was Mr. Harvey himself, with his thick-rimmed glasses and big, broad smile, sitting at his desk.

"Latasha! Ms. Gandy," he said, standing. "Great to see you both. Grab a snack and have a seat. We're waiting a few more minutes to start."

Behind the crowd, I spotted a handful of desks that had been pushed together with a tablecloth draped over them. They held a display of cookies and fresh fruit, plus a coffee urn.

"Oh, look!" Momma said. "Your favorite drink."

I responded with a playful scowl.

"Good thing Miss Prooper isn't running this show," I said quietly. I broke a cookie in half for Ella and folded a napkin around it. "She'd probably lock all the late people in the supply closet."

After a few more families arrived, Mr. Harvey stepped in front of his desk. "All right, it looks like everybody's here," he said. "Ladies, gents, hello and welcome to the Talent Pool. Some of you were part of the program last year, and some of you have had me for class, but for everyone who's new, I'm Mr. Harvey. I'm glad everyone could make it out this evening. In fact, kids, let's give our parents and guardians a big 'thank you' for making the time. And…a one-two-three!"

"Thank you," I chanted with the other kids.

"Perfection," Mr. Harvey said. "'Thank you's are important, because the Gifted and Talented team is not just made up of fourth and fifth graders. Your parents and guardians are part of the team, too. It's the grown-ups in our lives who give us rides to and from our events, who provide supplies, and who chip in for the snacks at our weekly meetings. By the way—a special thanks to Darla Washington and Mrs.

Washington, who provided our cookies and fruit tray tonight."

I glanced back at Darla and her grandma, who smiled and shrugged in unison as if they'd practiced it.

"To have the most successful year we can," Mr. Harvey continued, "we need everyone to work together. That's especially true when it comes to our big project: the Innovation Conversation. Now, the first round of judging—that's the regional round—takes place on Saturday, December fifteenth. That's the week after our Winter Band and Chorus concert, and the week before holiday break, so I hope we won't have any conflicts."

"I'll make sure I stay off the schedule," Momma whispered in my ear.

"December fifteenth might sound a long way off," Mr. Harvey said, "but anyone who was here last year can tell you: the I.C. adds up to be a whole *lot* of work."

The fifth grade families murmured in agreement.

"Last year, we *just* missed the cut to move on to the state round," Mr. Harvey said, holding his fingers an inch apart. "But the team did such great work. I think this could be our year, as long as we all stick together and do our part. What do you say, guys?

"Who's ready to get started?"

I knew I was! My hand shot up as high as I could reach. I saw other hands go up around me.

Mr. Harvey shook his head. "Uh-uh, we're not in school tonight," he said with a smile. "I want to hear you loud and proud! Who's ready?"

We all hollered together, even the grown-ups. Momma gripped my hand and grinned like she'd just been waiting for an excuse to shout. She looked so pretty when she lit up like that.

"All righty-roo!" Mr. Harvey said with a clap.

"Then onto our first order of business." He lifted a stack of stapled papers and passed them out.

"The contest judges just released the list of challenges we can choose from," he explained. "They all look interesting to me…but it's not up to me, or any of the other adults in the room. Whatever you kids pick to inspire your project is entirely up to you. So read everything over, and at next week's meeting I want to hear which challenge interests each of you the most. Then we'll vote on a winner."

"Latasha," Momma said as we walked, "you'll strain your eyes."

"The streetlights are super bright," I assured her, peering at the pages. We weren't even halfway home from the Talent Pool meeting, but I was already squinting at our challenge list.

"Our house lights are brighter," Momma said, taking the papers from my hands.

I huffed through my nose. Honestly, home was only ten minutes away, but I was just so psyched to get started!

When we got to our apartment, I grabbed the challenge list back from Momma. She went to the phone to check our voicemail, and Ella followed me to the kitchen table. I tried to read the papers over, but the pup kept nudging my side with her nose, sniffing and wagging.

I looked at Momma, who was listening to a message on the voicemail. "Momma," I said, "can you call her over?"

Momma held up a finger and kept listening on the phone. Something she heard made her roll her eyes and smile just the tiniest bit.

Ella kept prodding me, her tail whacking a table leg. "What!" I demanded, laughing. I patted the pocket she'd been sniffing and realized what she wanted. "Oh, sorry girl!" I'd totally forgotten about the half-cookie I'd set aside for her. She whined hungrily as I pulled the paper-wrapped treat from my pocket.

"I know, I know," I told her. "Your life is so hard." I broke up the cookie and fed Ella one nibble at a time as I studied the list of challenges. Mr. Harvey was right—they all looked interesting. One challenge was about planning a trip to the moon, but we could only bring certain supplies. Another one wanted us to put on a show about an old explorer and his adventures. The third one especially caught my eye. For that challenge, we had to put on our own musical where all of the characters were animals.

"How about that one?" I asked Ella as she chewed a cookie bite. "Maybe I could play you!"

Momma set the phone down in front of me on the table.

"You have a message," she said, walking toward the living room.

"Who, Ricky?"

"Oh, no," she replied, exaggerating each word. "It was *the president*!"

I looked after Momma as she left the kitchen. The president? Of what? And what had gotten her so grumpy all of a sudden?

I turned on the phone and went to our voicemail. Its lady-robot voice told me we had one new message. When it began, though, I didn't hear anyone speaking—I heard a piano! It took me a moment to recognize the song. It was "Hail to the Chief," except it sounded quicker and jazzier than when we'd listened to it during social studies. Then the song stopped and a voice began to speak.

"Hello," it said, "this is the president of the United States calling for Ms. Latasha Esther…"

My mouth opened in a wide O. The *actual president?* What on Earth was going on? I stared down at Ella, but believe it or not, she wasn't much help. I pressed the phone close to my ear.

"Latasha," the president said, "on behalf of the United States government, I would like to personally offer you an apology. You might think that your father has forgotten about you, but I assure you, that is not at all the case. He has been busy this month working for me, the president, on a top-secret musical mission. Sadly, the details are classified. But now that your dad—who, by the way, is one of the bravest and most handsome men I've ever met…"

I began to realize that this voice sounded not at all like the president, and a whole bunch like someone else I knew. "Daddy…" I said, groaning and laughing at the same time.

His message went on, "Now that the world is once again safe, I've given your father permission to visit you. He will be coming to Pittsburgh this Saturday. Latasha, if you would still like to see him, he would very much like to see you. Please call him at home. God bless you, and God bless the United States of America."

And then "Hail to the Chief" picked up again until the message ended. I was smiling so hard that my cheeks tingled. I set down the phone and looked at Ella. "I tell you what, pup," I said, rapping my fingers against the challenge list on the table. "He gets a 'ten' for style."

Chapter Six

Kidd On Keys

"Natasha, don't get me wrong," Momma began. "I'm happy you wanted to clean the house. But did you really need to clean Ella, too?"

"First impressions are very important," I replied, wrestling with my towel-clad pup.

Ella hadn't been dirty or stinky—actually, her dog food makes her fur smell like a corn chip, and, for whatever reason, her paws always smell like buttery popcorn. But I wanted her to look groomer-fresh when Dad came over today.

That's right—it was actually going to happen! After I'd heard Dad's message on Thursday, I talked to Momma and she called him that very night. They agreed that he would come by at two p.m. on Saturday so that we could spend the afternoon together. I'd been counting down the hours ever since.

Counting down the hours and cleaning every inch of our apartment. I'd dusted the ceiling fans, cleared every cobweb, and I even had Mrs. Okocho come upstairs to teach me her "secret floor-mopping technique" for the kitchen. It turned out her "big secret" was just to do it twice—boring! At least it kept me busy, though. Waiting around is the worst.

That was my other reason for bathing Ella, even though she doesn't much like baths—I knew that with bribing her to climb into the tub, actually washing her, and drying her off, that last hour until two o'clock would zip right on by.

Ella's bath had gone as planned, except for one detail that I'd forgotten. Maybe our towels are scratchy, or maybe it's static buildup—but whenever I try to dry Ella off, she goes bonkers! So now, right at the time Dad was supposed to arrive, instead of an adorable, sort-of-corn-chip-smelling cutie, I had a drippy, wriggly beast on my hands.

Or, to be more precise, in my arms. She was struggling with all her might to break free from my towel grip and zoom around the whole house. That was the way she preferred to dry off.

"Settle!" I insisted as I rubbed her coat. "What will your grandpa think?"

"Grandpa, huh?" asked Momma from the door.

"Sure," I replied. "He's my dad, and she's my girl… so, Ella's his grand-pup."

"I'm sure he'll love that," Momma said with a chuckle. She paused, thinking. "Do you…tell her that I'm her grandma?"

I shot Momma a *Really?* kind of look. "Well, yeah."

Momma backed out of the doorway, waving her arms like she was running away. "Oh, I feel old."

"Let's keep that grandma-grandpa talk just between you and me," I told Ella. I stroked her side and her wriggling slowed.

But then the doorbell rang. "He's here!" I exclaimed. Ella tore free and raced for the door. She was so excited, though, that she tried to run out sideways and banged right into the doorframe.

"You poor little simpleton," I giggled as she shook the water from her coat and rushed out of the bathroom.

I followed Ella's damp paw prints into the kitchen. I found her next to Momma, flapping her ears against her head to dry them. "I'll go down for the door," Momma said. "Put her on the leash or something!"

That seemed wise. I didn't want my pup jumping all over Dad until they knew each other better.

I hooked my fingers under Ella's collar and let Momma slip out the door. "Come on," I pleaded, clipping on her leash. "You want a Teddy Snack?" No response. "Dessert?" That at least got me a pause. But then two sets of feet thumped up the hall stairs and

Ella set right back to dancing. To be honest, though, I really couldn't blame her. If I had a tail, I'd have been wagging it like crazy, too!

Momma reopened our door. And there he was behind her. He wasn't quite as tall as I remembered—taller than Momma, still, but not like the picture in my head. Everything else was the same, though. He smiled, thin-lipped, like he was thinking of a joke. His brown eyes took in every detail of the room as he entered. His thick, wavy hair, orange-red like a fireball, peeked out from under his hat brim.

His eyes fell to me and his thin smile grew until his teeth began to show. I recognized that smile—it looked like mine.

"Hey there, pumpkin," he said.

I barely noticed Ella bumping the side of my knee. I wanted to run over screaming and wrap my dad in a huge hug—and I also wanted to give him a good punch in the thigh for making me wait so long. Instead, I just stood my ground and smiled back, hoping he'd notice that we matched. "Hey, Daddy," I said quietly.

He looked down at Ella and purposely widened his eyes. "Well now!" he said, stepping past Momma. "This must be the infamous Lady Ella!" He glanced at me. "May I say hello?"

I nodded eagerly and loosened my grip on Ella's leash. She pranced toward him, spinning and hopping, and Dad dropped to one knee to pet her. "She's a little wet," I warned.

"That I can handle," he said, offering the back of his hand so she could learn his scent. Then Dad removed his hat with a grand gesture. "It is a sincere pleasure and honor to be in your presence," he told Ella, bowing his head almost to her eye level.

Ella twisted around and whacked him right across the face with her tail. Dad flinched back in shock and I yanked Ella away as quickly as I could.

"Well," he said, blinking the sting away, "that smarts."

"You okay?" asked Momma, laughing. I wasn't laughing, though, not one bit. I wanted to run to my room and hide under the covers until my father gave up and went home. I didn't know if I could feel any guiltier than I did in that moment.

Then a drop of blood fell from Dad's nose and onto the twice-mopped floor.

"Still get these when you're nervous?" asked Momma, glancing at the tissues up Dad's nostrils.

"Sometimes," Dad replied, watching the ceiling. With those tissues stuffed in his nose, he sounded like he was half-man, half-kazoo. "Not so often anymore."

"I am so, so sorry, Daddy," I said. I was doing everything I could not to cry. Our whole afternoon together had been ruined before it could even start. Because of Ella, he'd spent the last fifteen minutes stuck staring at our kitchen ceiling. I'd have drunk a whole pitcher of icky black coffee if it would take back what she'd done.

But Dad just looked over at me and winked. "It's only a trickle."

"Keep your head back," Momma ordered, guiding him by his forehead.

"Yes, Nurse Gandy," he said with a flare of his eyebrows.

"Not quite," she corrected, and then she looked over toward me. "Hey, honey? Why don't you go check on the pup? I'll bet she feels terrible."

Ella had done exactly what I'd wanted to do: run away and hide in my room. I found her curled up at the head of my bed, tucked into the corner behind my pillow. It was almost cute enough to make me forgive her on the spot.

But not quite. "Ella Fitzgerald Gandy, I am very

disappointed in you," I told her, my voice heavy and slow. "You almost broke your grandpa's face. That was bad. Very bad. Don't you want to have a grandpa?" For a second I forgot what I meant to say next, but then it came back. "You will sit here while I'm gone and think about what you did."

And then I grabbed my notebook off my desk and left the room. Ella must have realized how serious I was, because she did the unimaginable and stayed right where I'd told her to.

Before I entered the kitchen, I heard Momma and Dad talking, so I waited outside to listen.

"Am I all cleaned up?" asked Dad. His voice had returned to normal, so I guessed his nosebleed had stopped and the tissues were out.

"Yeah, you look good," Momma replied. The sink turned on for a second, then back off.

"So do you, you know," Dad said.

"Oh, you drop that nonsense, mister," Momma told him, but she didn't sound mean.

"No fooling," Dad said. "You look great. Both of you."

I smiled beside the doorway. Maybe the day wasn't ruined after all.

"And come on in, Latasha," Momma called out. "I know you're out there."

Rats—how did Momma *do* that? I came in and saw my parents standing beside each other at the sink. Dad stepped forward, took a deep breath, and put his hat firmly on his head. "So, kiddo," he said, "we ready to hit the town?"

"As long as you're not mad," I said uncertainly.

"You kidding?" he replied. "I got beat up by Ella Fitzgerald! That's like a badge of honor."

Some people call Pittsburgh the City of Bridges, because we have about a million of them. But I think it should be called the City of Neighborhoods. Pittsburgh isn't one big place—it's really a bunch of little places. Within the city limits, there are ninety different neighborhoods. I'm not even exaggerating that number. I counted it once, right on a map in the library. Just don't ask me to list all of their names.

Anyway, that's the reason a real Pittsburgher won't tell you she's from Pittsburgh. She'll say she's from Lawrenceville. She'll say she's from Polish Hill. As for me, I'm from Friendship. The cool thing about having so many neighborhoods, with all their crooked lines and one-way streets, is that every time you leave your own, it feels like an adventure.

The only problem is that if you don't know exactly where you're going, it's super easy to get lost.

Like Dad and I were now.

"We're almost there," he insisted. "I can feel it in my bones." We were rumbling in Dad's powder-blue station wagon down a street I'd never heard of.

"Where are we going again?" I asked.

"This cool coffee shop my buddy brought me to last year," he replied. "It's in…Beltzhoover…near the park."

I sighed. Describing a place as "near the park" was about as helpful as saying it was "near the bridge."

The brakes squeaked as we stopped at a light. Dad looked at me. "What do you say?" he asked. "Left turn?"

I shrugged. "Could be," I said, nervously tapping my vocabulary notebook in my lap. I had listed so many questions for Dad in it, but if the day kept up like it had been, I wouldn't get a chance to ask any of them.

Dad noticed my drumming. "What do you have there?" he asked. "Diary?"

"Sort of," I said. I explained how I used the notebook to write down my thoughts and cool words that I wanted to remember for later.

"It's funny," Dad replied. "I used to do something

a lot like that."

I perked up in my seat. "Really?"

"Sure," he said, "except mine was all rhymes. Big lists of rhyming words, you know, for when I'd write lyrics? Except my notebook didn't have a cool little strap like yours to keep it shut."

I smiled. I liked how Dad noticed little details about things, just like I did.

"I write other things in here, too," I said. "Like, I wrote a whole page of questions I wanted to ask you."

"Oh-ho," he said, chuckling. "So our little get together was going to be a—what? An interrogation?"

I blushed. "No, not like that," I said. "More like an interview."

"Ah, I get you." He turned onto another street. "Well, since we are hopelessly lost at the moment, why don't we start the interview now?"

I happily opened my notebook, pulling the strap an extra bit so it would make the little *snap* that I liked. I flipped through the book to my interview page. "All right," I said. "Question one—"

"Lay it on me, sister!" he shouted.

"Question one," I repeated firmly, hoping to keep the silliness in check. "What instrument do you play?"

Dad looked at me like I'd spoken in Japanese.

"Your mother never told you?" he asked.

The hurt in his voice made me nervous. "No…" I said cautiously.

"Well," he said, pausing for far too long. I watched his jaw muscles flex. "Well, why would it come up, I guess? Never mind. Just, uh, look behind you—under the blanket."

I turned my head. On the backseat, a dark blanket covered a large, rectangular object. I strained to grab the blanket, but my seat belt held me in place. "I can't reach," I told him.

"Don't tell your mother I did this," Dad said, and before I could reply, he unclicked my seat belt. "Just a quick peek."

I swiftly leaned and yanked the blanket. Underneath was a huge, shining keyboard that reached from door to door. "Whoa!" I said. I wanted to give it a long look and figure out what all of the knobs and buttons up above the keys were for—but I was nervous about not wearing my seat belt, so I faced front and re-buckled myself. "So was that you playing 'Hail to the Chief' on that message?" I asked. "You're good!"

Dad half-smiled, but I could tell that he was thinking about something else. He was squinting like he was trying to make out something very far away.

"Daddy?" I asked.

His head jerked toward me. "Listen," he said. "Let's put this coffee shop on hold."

I didn't even know what had gone wrong. "But…" I couldn't let the day end like this, I just couldn't. My breath caught in my throat and I felt the corner of my lip quiver.

"How about french fries instead?" asked Dad.

My heart started beating again.

"Do you like french fries?" he asked.

I had to think for a second so that I could remember how to speak. "Yeah, I do!"

"I know a place," Dad told me. He pulled into a gas station to turn the car around. "And even better…I actually know where it is."

"Welcome to the Dirty O," Dad announced as we entered through the door. Then he saw the look on my face and burst out laughing. "Relax, kid, it's just a nickname. It's perfectly safe."

Looking around the shop, with its scuffed-up tile and the grubby college kids at almost every table, I understood the nickname completely. What I didn't understand was why we'd come here.

"We're here for the best fries in town!" Dad explained. "I used to come here when I was at Pitt." He meant the University of Pittsburgh, the biggest college in the city.

Dad took me to a counter in the back. A lady with bushy gray hair and a huge mole beside her nose asked us for our order. "You want to split a small?" Dad asked me.

"Can we get a medium?" I asked. I'd been so busy cleaning the house that I'd totally forgotten about lunch.

"Look up before you decide," he said. He pointed to the wall above the counter, which had different-sized paper food boats nailed to it. "Those are the sizes."

I stared at the writing on each boat. *Small* was the size of a paperback novel. *Medium* was the size of an encyclopedia. And *Large* was the size of the Carnegie Library.

"Small's okay," I said.

Dad laughed hard—he has this great, really-real laugh that shakes his head and his shoulders—and then he ordered us a small. After we paid and got an order number, Dad picked a table for us in the corner. "After you, madame," he said, holding out my chair. I could definitely get used to that.

"So," Dad said, dropping into his seat, "want to move on through the interview?"

I scanned through my notebook past the questions we'd covered. Such as: *How old are you?* (Thirty-two.) *When's your birthday?* (June third.) *Do you have any siblings?* (I'm an "only," like you.)

"Here we go," I said, touching my pen to a new line. "Do you have a band?"

"Not exactly," Dad replied. "I like to play all over. So I just sit in wherever I'm needed. It's good being the guy who fills in—you're like the hero of the band."

"Is that what you're doing tonight?" I asked. "Filling in?"

"With this jazz and soul outfit," he agreed. "They're called the Ministers. Their piano player's an older guy—got some problems with his health. So to the rescue, here I come…" His fingers danced across the table's edge and flashed up like they were taking off in flight. "*The Kidd on Keys.*"

"Is that what people call you?"

Dad shrugged. "It's what *I* call me, anyway," he said. "My nickname with most folks is, *Hey, you're late!*"

We both laughed—but I could kind of see their point.

"What's next?" he asked. "This is fun."

I moved on to my next question. "What are your parents like?"

Dad pulled in a big breath through his nose. "Pop died when I was a kid," he said. "I was in junior high."

"Just like Momma was," I said quietly. The thought made my eyes sting.

"Well," Dad jumped in, "I do still have my mum."

I had a grandma! "Does she live nearby?" I asked eagerly.

"Oh, no," he said, "not for a few years now."

I huffed in disappointment.

"She got remarried a while back, retired down to South Florida," he said. "I go down to see her for a few days every Thanksgiving. And *that* is about enough for the both of us."

I gaped at him—I couldn't imagine seeing Momma only once a year.

"Mum is—" Dad said, pausing. "I love my mum. But she always thinks she knows what's best, and she always takes the time to *tell you*. She has this way of talking down that makes you feel smaller—like she shrunk you with her words. I'd just as soon keep my distance."

I wanted to ask why she was like that, but a glass-shattering screech cut me off.

"Number fifty-eight!" shouted the lady with the

mole by her nose. For a half of a second, it killed every conversation in the restaurant.

"Was that us?" Dad said in a fake whisper. "I didn't hear her."

I liked the way Dad laughed, but there was something I liked even better—the way he made me laugh.

He handed me our order ticket. "Grab that, would you? And napkins. We'll need 'em."

I got our fries from the counter and when I came back, Dad's fingers were dancing along our table's edge again like it was a keyboard. He was nodding and his upper body swayed to a soundless beat. It made me think of this one lady in our church choir who gets all the solos—when she sings, she does it with her whole body.

"Are you working out a new song?" I asked.

Dad's eyes opened. "All the time," he replied.

"That's how I feel about stories," I said. "Everywhere I look, I see one."

Dad smiled. "You got anything cooking right now?"

"I'm kind of wondering about the fry counter lady," I said. When I'd gone to get our food, I'd spotted her near the fryers, talking with the cook—he was this bone-skinny guy with a gray ponytail tucked into his hairnet. "I think she and the cook are having a secret romance."

"Is that so?" he said with a laugh. "How'd you pick that up?"

It was all in how the lady was acting with him. "They were laughing and then she touched his arm," I explained. "But when she did it, she glanced around like she hoped no one else had noticed."

Dad grabbed the brim of his hat and tipped it toward me. "I like your brain, kid, you know that?"

That might have been the best compliment I'd ever gotten.

He shifted his hat back into place and leaned across our tray. "I have a little tale for you," he said offhandedly, "and it's absolutely true. If you're interested."

I nodded fiercely. "Tell it!"

Dad pointed at me in agreement. "This story takes place about eleven years back, on a chilly October evening," he said. "My senior year at Pitt. First semester, just past midterms. The setting? Right…here."

"At the Dirty O?" I asked.

Dad flashed his eyebrows devilishly. "At this very table."

I pulled my chair in until I could feel the table

against my ribs.

"The characters of this tale are: myself—"

"*—the Kidd on Keys—*"

"—and, believe it or not…the lady at the fry counter."

"The secret romance?" I asked, glancing back. She was leaning against the cash register, still chatting it up with the cook.

"Well," Dad said, "she looked a lot different back then. She was a lot more slender, for one. Young, with a beautiful face—and the smoothest skin you ever did see."

I smirked at him. To be honest, it made me a little queasy to hear him talk like that about some random stranger.

But Dad went on. "She had a much deeper tan back in those days," he said. "And the sweetest voice. Honey-sweet."

That left me baffled—the counter lady's voice was all vinegar.

Dad tucked a strand of hair behind his ear. "And she had a cute…perfectly round…afro."

"Dad!" I burst out. "What kind of weird story is this?"

He shot me a crafty grin. "This is where I met your mother."

In an instant, the Dirty O was transformed. Its looks were unchanged, but it somehow felt like an entirely new place. I'm not sure what expression I was wearing—but it must have been the right one, because Dad leaned back in satisfaction and went on with the story.

"Like I mentioned, it was my last year of school. I took classes during the day and played with anyone who'd let me on stage at night. And in between, I was coming here a few times a week for a nice, balanced meal of…french fries." I snickered—Dad knew just how long to pause to give his jokes a punch. "Speaking of! Have some. They're good as leftovers, but better fresh."

We each popped a salty fry in our mouths. Dad was right—they were the best I'd ever tasted.

"So I'm coming here pretty regular," he continued. "Then one night, that cold October night, there's a new girl working the counter."

"Momma," I said.

"She doesn't pay me much mind at first," he said, dipping a fry in ketchup, "but I sure notice her. She's always humming songs behind the counter. Old stuff—*good* stuff. Dusty Springfield, Etta James— and, of course, the indispensible Ms. Fitzgerald."

He jabbed our table with a pointer finger. "I start

sitting here in the corner so I can hear her better. And, I'll admit, so I can see her better, too. Soon, I start giving her flyers for the shows where I'm playing. Every time I'm in here, a new flyer. A basement party on Atwood, a club gig at the Upstage. And she's always got an excuse for why she can't make it. One time, she tells me she doesn't have money to throw away on a show. So I try to play it all cool and I tell her, 'I'll get your name onto the list.' You know what she said?"

"What?" I asked.

He raised the pitch of his voice and said, "*How about I put you on the list? The list of white boys who come in here pestering me for a date.*"

That was Momma, all right—he'd even cocked his head like she does when she's annoyed.

"But that didn't stop me," Dad said. "I just realized I'd have to be a bit more creative."

"So what'd you do?" I asked.

"I made her a CD," he replied. "A CD with all the songs I'd heard her humming at the counter."

"You remembered them all?"

He looked me right in the eye. "How could I forget?"

Why hadn't Momma ever said anything about all this? It was more romantic than any of those silly fairy tales we used to read together. "Did she like the CD?" I asked.

That grin that matched mine spread across Dad's face. "Oh, yeah," he said. "And that was that. She was done for."

We talked for another hour as we finished our fries. Dad didn't share much more about Grandma, but he told me all about his adventures playing on the road. I told him about school, and Mr. Harvey, and how I wanted to put on that animal musical for the Innovation Conversation. And we laughed a whole year's worth of laughter.

On our ride back to Friendship, though, it was Dad's story about Momma that really stuck with me. It made me wonder, *If they were such a good match, why'd they ever split up?* Only one reason came to mind—and it made me feel so bad that I pushed it away before my brain could really think it.

We pulled up to the curb on Graham Street. "Wish me luck tonight," Dad said, and I did.

"Can we do this again soon?" I asked. "Like, really soon?"

"Without a doubt, my dear," he said. "If you do end up doing that musical project for the…"

"Innovation Conversation," I chimed in.

"If you do that," he said, "maybe I can give you some song tips."

That settled it—I'd fight for that project even if it meant taking on the whole Talent Pool!

"Do you want to come up and say hi to Momma?" I asked.

"Not today," he said. "But I've got something you can take with you." He reached back under his keyboard and grabbed a recordable CD in a plastic case.

I stared at the disc. "Is that…the mix you made for Momma?"

"I made this one for you," he replied.

My eyebrows shot all the way up to my hairline!

"I didn't know before if it would fit you," he went on, "but I think I did all right. The playlist is in the back of the case. It's all female singers. Check the title."

Dad had written it on the disc in marker: *Tough Ladies for My Tough Lady.*

I raced up into the house so that I could listen to my new CD. But first I had to contend with my crazy leaping dog. She was so excited to see me that she wrapped her forepaws around my arm and wouldn't let go.

"I'm here, my girl, I'm here," I told her, holding the disc out of her reach.

"Thank goodness," Momma said as she entered the kitchen. "That dog cried for an hour after you left!"

"She did?" I asked, instantly guilty.

"She must've thought you weren't coming back or something," Momma replied. "She was inconsolable."

I knelt and embraced Ella around the waist with one arm. "Poor simple girl," I whispered to her. "The loneliest dog in the world."

"So how'd it go?" asked Momma.

I sped through a summary of our afternoon. Momma's face was tough to read through it all—but to be honest, I wasn't trying very hard. I just wanted to listen to my mix!

"He made you a CD," Momma commented.

"Just like for you," I replied.

Momma sucked her cheeks in, just nodding to herself.

"I'm going to my room to listen," I said. "You want me to leave my door open?"

"Closed is fine," she said.

Even better! Ella and I went to my room and shut the door. I had an old CD player that used to belong to Momma in my desk drawer and a pair of small speakers for it—not too loud, but definitely good enough. I hooked everything up, popped Dad's CD in, and let it play.

From the first song on, I was hooked. Some of his "tough ladies" I'd heard of, like Mary J. Blige and Adele. But most of the names on the playlist were new to me—someone named Mavis Staples; some super-sad, super-beautiful singer named Nina Simone; another called Janis Joplin. The songs' styles were all over the map, but each singer had one thing in common: it was like each one was talking straight to me.

Ella watched me from the bed. "He's not a musician," I told her as I swayed on my feet. "He's a magician."

Chapter Seven
Ella's Anniversary

Anyone who's spent five minutes with Ella knows that she can be a handful—or an armful, or a lapful, or a licky-face-tail-whack-to-the-kneesful. But there is one place where she behaves like a regular angel: in Mrs. Okocho's Oldsmobile. As soon as she climbs onto the bedsheet Mrs. Okocho always spreads across the back seat for her, Ella just curls up in a ball and doesn't stir until we reach our destination. I never trained her to do that. I don't know how she picked it up.

What I do know is this: as we all rode to Dr. Vanderstam's office, I found myself wishing that Ella's calm was contagious.

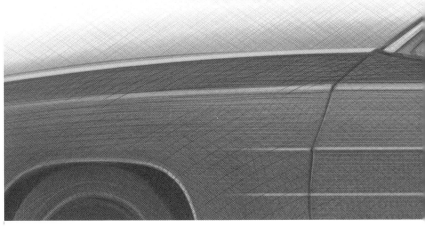

It was the third Saturday in October, and Mrs. Okocho, Momma, and I were taking Ella for an important check-up. A year ago this week, Ella had had her accident and her surgery. Now it was time for Dr. Vanderstam to examine her and learn how the rest of her body had held up.

I always got a little nervous when we took Ella to the vet, but today I kept finding new things to fret over. What if Dr. Vanderstam said I was giving her too many treats and making her fat? Or what if he told me I wasn't giving her enough exercise? Or that I was giving her *too much* exercise?

"You can't give a dog too much exercise," Momma assured me, looking over her shoulder.

"You totally can," I replied. It was true—I'd looked it up online. "And for a dog with three legs, it can lead to this horrible thing called…arthritis."

Momma and Mrs. Okocho shared a glance and a smirk, which I did not appreciate one bit!

"It's a serious condition!" I cried. "Your joints wear out and feel all swollen—"

"—Honey, please," Momma cut in. "Everything will be fine, I promise you."

"Listen to your mama," Mrs. Okocho said. "She is a wise lady."

"And then later today," Momma added, "you'll have a nice visit with your father, and you'll wow him with your world-famous meatball hoagies."

I lowered my eyes to my lap, grinning. "They're not world-famous."

"Give it time," Momma replied with a wink.

I had to admit, meatball hoagies *were* sort of my specialty—even if they made up a full one-quarter of the things I knew how to cook. I couldn't wait to see the look on Dad's face when he tried one. As long as Ella's check-up went well, I knew that today would be a perfect day.

I reached over to my round fur ball and stroked her shoulders. Now that I thought about it, I'd had a lot of great days lately. The last six weeks had been a breeze—all along the way, things had just seemed to find a way of working out how I wanted.

It all started with Talent Pool, that first week after Dad's visit.

"Hear ye, hear ye!" Mr. Harvey announced. "The first official meeting of the Cedarville Elementary Gifted and Talented Club is now in session!" He leaned back against his desk and clapped his hands together. "Let's pick a challenge."

Each of us had a turn to argue for our favorite idea. I got to go first—"Since you've got your hand a mile in the air," Mr. Harvey noted. I quickly explained why I thought the musical challenge would be best. I talked about all of the different creative skills we'd use to make costumes and backdrops, and what fun it would be to tell a story with songs, and how our show would have the most style in the whole competition.

"Plus," I added, "I've already got an idea for an animal song—it's called 'The Lonely Dog Blues.'"

You can probably guess who'd inspired that.

Sometimes I get nervous talking in front of a group like that, but I felt great once I'd finished. A few kids hopped on board with me right off the bat.

But still, some kids had other challenges in mind. Two boys especially—these fifth graders named Russell and Gautam—had their hearts set on doing the Mission to Mars challenge. In true science fair style, they'd even made a poster board about why it was the strongest choice. It was nerdy—but I wished I'd thought of it!

"The last three teams to win our region did projects about science," Russell argued.

"We could act out a skit about landing on Mars," Gautam said.

Then they did their big finish—they unveiled a slow-motion walk they'd invented that made them look like they were in low gravity on Mars.

I worried that those boys might win the group over—but then I got backup from an unexpected place.

"May I speak, Mr. Harvey?" It was Darla Washington.

"Miss Washington has the floor," he declared.

Darla cleared her throat in her usual dramatic way. "I've had a lot of hobbies," she said, "and I'm pretty good at most of them."

Oh boy, I thought. Darla has this habit of talking very highly of herself—sometimes for minutes at a time. I slid down in my seat and tried not to sigh too loudly.

"But my favorite hobby is playing the piano," she said. With that, I straightened up in my chair and leaned forward. "My grandma's had me in lessons since I was three, and I've gotten first place ribbons at my last two recitals. It would be so much fun to play for a musical. I'll bet that between my playing and Latasha's writing, we could put on a show that no one would forget!"

My cheeks were burning hot—partly because I was flattered, and partly because I felt guilty for thinking she only wanted to brag.

Darla wasn't done, though. She went on to tell each other kid in the club how his or her talents would help make a great musical—how Donnie Yerba could paint scenery, and how Rachel Kwan could make animal ears for our costumes.

"And science could be important, too," she said. "We'll have to do lots of studying to make sure we get each animal just right. Maybe we'll even find one that moves like this!"

And then she did a perfect imitation of Russell and Gautam's Mars walk.

Darla basically saved the day—when it came time to vote, only Russell stuck with the Mission to Mars challenge. In the end, Gautam jumped spaceship to give the animal musical a total of eleven votes.

Well, twelve votes if you count both of my hands.

We came up with a story idea very quickly. It was all about what happens when the owners go away and their pets get left home alone. Our characters were some hamsters who want to eat all of the cereal in the house, two cats who think that the humans are *their* pets, a tattletale parakeet—and, of course, one very lonely dog.

Since we didn't have a ton of time, we decided to take the team's favorite songs and just change the words to be about animals. That made it easy for me to come up with lyrics and for Darla to learn each tune. But when it came to "The Lonely Dog Blues," I didn't want to copy a song that was already out there. I wanted to do something unique. And I knew just who I needed to help me.

Fortunately, Dad seemed really excited to teach me about music. "That sick keys player is going to be taking a long rest," he said, "so I'll already be down your way quite a bit. You've got great timing, kid!" I always got a happy little smile when he called me *kid*—it was different from how Dad's name is spelled, but sometimes I pretended that it was the same.

Over the past six weeks, Dad had come to see me three times. The first day, we went out to do what he called "invaluable musical research." Really, all Dad did was take me to his favorite used record store in town. It wasn't just called a record store, either—it actually sold real records, like the vinyl kind that you have to play on a turntable. It was fun because I got to listen to strange songs over the store's crackly speakers, and I learned a bunch of new words—like *sleeve*, which is the thin paper case for a record, and *platter*, which is what people used to call records because of how big they are.

Dad even promised he'd buy me anything I wanted that was under ten dollars—which would have been awesome if we actually had a record player at home. I tried to take it as one of those it's-the-thought-that-counts moments, like the time Mrs. Okocho made me a Christmas sweater with a puff-paint snowman on it.

That afternoon had been fun, but Dad's other two visits had been more useful. On those days, we didn't go anywhere—Dad came to the house, lugged his keyboard up the stairs, and gave me music lessons. Momma hadn't exactly been thrilled by the idea at first, but she gave in once I explained how much it would help the Talent Pool.

Our first lesson was about chords, which are the note clusters you use to build a song. Our second lesson was about the ways you can arrange chords next to each other, which are called *progressions*. Dad had a great way of explaining it to me. "Chords are like words," he said. "They only tell a story if you put them in the right order."

At the end of that lesson, we'd made plans for today. "Next time I come down," Dad had told me, while collapsing his keyboard stand, "I'll reveal to you the secrets of the jazz universe. We're going to learn the twelve-bar blues."

Even though I was worried—sorry, *concerned*—about Ella's check-up, I could hardly wait to see Dad. I really wanted to show off all the work I'd done for our animal musical. All of the lyrics were written, from "The Lonely Dog Blues" to Darla's personal favorite, "Hamster" (in the style of Aretha Franklin). But even more, I was excited because today's visit was different from all the others.

Until today, Dad and I had only met up when he already had a gig in town. But this afternoon he didn't have a gig, with the Ministers or anyone else. He was driving down just because I'd invited him. He was supposed to arrive at one for our lesson and then stay all the way through dinner. When I'd asked him to join us, he gave me the best answer. He'd said, "There is no place I'd rather eat." That even made Momma smile.

But before I could enjoy our perfect family dinner, I had to survive Ella's check-up.

Ella's tail slapped the doorframe as she led Momma, Mrs. Okocho, and me into the waiting room. At the desk, Miss Simon set down the magazine she was reading and smiled at us. "There's that happy tail!" she said. "And how've the Gandys been?"

"Fabulous," I told her.

"Did you ever get things worked out with that neighbor dog?" she asked.

"It's all okay now," I replied.

"I'm quite glad to hear it!" Miss Simon said. "Dr. V will be ready for you in a minute."

We sat in chairs along the wall. Mrs. Okocho unfolded the comics section from her morning newspaper. I petted Ella to keep her settled. And Momma put a hand on my shoulder—almost like she was settling me.

While we waited, I thought about my pup and Hamlet. I'd told Miss Simon the truth—those two got along now almost as well as Ricky and I did. But lately, I hadn't been the best about setting up play dates. Between Dad's visits, homework, and especially Talent Pool, I hadn't had any time to bring her over. Thinking back, I hadn't even sat at Ricky's lunch table much in the past few weeks—I'd been eating with Darla and some other Talent Pool kids so we could brainstorm song ideas. I wondered if Ella missed her easygoing pal.

Before I could think more about it, though, a lanky figure in a white lab coat entered from the exam area. "Come on back to room one," Dr. Vanderstam said.

Momma and I stood, and I took her hand as we walked Ella back. "I will stay here and read my funny papers," Mrs. Okocho said.

Ella wiggled along as we went back. She liked Dr. Vanderstam a lot—which was good, since he had to poke around all over while he examined her. He was able to check places that Ella didn't even like me to touch, like inside her ears. My pup just smiled and panted as she stood on the metal exam table. As Dr. Vanderstam studied Ella, I studied him, trying to figure out what every nod, *hmm*, and *ahh* really meant.

Within a few minutes, the exam was over. Dr.

Vanderstam smiled and announced, "Miss Fitzgerald is in perfect health."

I blinked in disbelief. "She is?"

He patted Ella's back, which set her to wagging. "Her coat has filled in nicely around her scar, her muscles are strong, her weight is healthy, and her joints are in fine condition," Dr. Vanderstam said. Ella's tail caught his lab coat, whacking a flap into the air. The vet flinched and laughed at the same time. "I can tell she's in wonderful hands."

Momma kissed me on the top of the head.

We all left the exam room and Momma went to Miss Simon's desk to write a check for the visit. "All is well?" asked Mrs. Okocho.

"That's right," I said, relieved and surprised at the same time.

We rode home in the Oldsmobile, Ella's body on the bedsheet and her head in my lap. I rubbed my jaw—it felt all hot and worn out, like I'd eaten a whole bag of beef jerky. "My mouth kind of hurts," I said.

Momma glanced back. "Well," she said, "you *were* grinding your teeth that whole visit."

"I can't believe I worried so much over nothing," I muttered.

"Don't beat yourself up," Momma replied. She turned toward me like she had a secret to share.

"Worrying over nothing is half a mom's job."

I cuddled against my pup. When Momma treats me like we're partners, I feel like the most important girl in the world.

At home, I did one last check in the kitchen for all of my dinner supplies. Once I was double-sure that we had everything, I grabbed our fresh hoagie buns from the counter and tucked them away on a high shelf. "Don't even think about thieving," I told Ella.

And then I waited for Dad. I flipped through a couple of books on my shelf. I tried singing my girl the opening I'd written for "The Lonely Dog Blues":

"If you want to stay smiling,
Then don't you look at me.
I'm the saddest little puppy
That you ever did see…"

At a quarter past one, Momma poked in to check on me. "How are you girls holding up?" she asked.

"He's always a little late," I told Momma.

That was true—but as the minutes ticked away, Dad became more than a little late. Soon enough, it was two o'clock, and we still hadn't heard a single word from him. My antsy feet had practically tapped a hole in the floor—and I was feeling more foolish by the second. Ella paced across my legs on the bed, brushing against me like she did when a storm was coming.

It made sense for Ella to behave that way. Though the sky outside my window was clear and brilliant blue, I could see a storm coming. And its name was Momma.

Her grumbles were like distant thunder as she stalked past my door.

"…Same old Patrick…"

"…no-account fool thinks…"

"...another thing coming!"

I knew Momma just wanted to stick up for me, but seeing her angry only made me feel worse. It was such a relief when the phone rang a few minutes later.

I hurried to the kitchen, but Momma beat me to the receiver. "Hello?"

"Is it Daddy?" I asked.

Momma held up a rigid finger. "Oh!" she said, breaking into an icy smile. "You want to speak with your *daughter*. I'm so glad you didn't forget about your *daughter*."

I turned my head away as she handed over the phone. I hated how Momma looked when she got mean. It made me nervous that someday she'd point that look at me.

I put the phone to my ear. "Hey, Daddy."

"Kid," he began, and from the careful, sighing way he said it, I knew what would come next.

"You can't make it," I replied.

"I am a Class-A jerk," he said.

I sank back against the wall. I saw Momma standing in the living room. She was pinching the bridge of her nose and shaking her head slightly.

"I should have called before now," Dad said. "I should have called this morning, the moment I got the gig. But I got wrapped up and—"

"—What gig?"

"This wedding out in central PA," he replied. "Buddy of mine called me to help out, last minute. I'm driving over now. I'm really sorry to do this to you."

Then don't! I wanted to scream.

"But we had plans," I said instead. I sounded like a mouse.

"I have to take whatever comes, whenever it comes," he replied. "It's just how this line of work is. Do you understand?"

I didn't understand, not the littlest bit. How could he drop me, just like that? I held the receiver away from my mouth so he wouldn't hear me sniffle.

"I'll take a rain check on our lesson," Dad went on. "I promise."

"And dinner, too?" I asked, my voice all wobbly.

"Sure, definitely," he said.

I breathed out slowly, hoping that would make my heart stop racing.

"I need you to know," Dad said, "I'd really rather spend time with you right now."

"You mean it?"

"Heck, yeah!" he cried. "Don't you know how much fun you are?"

That didn't lift my bad feelings away, but it made them lighter—light enough that I could smile.

"But it's like I said," he added. "If I want to keep my head above water, I've got to grab on to whatever little driftwood blows my way. Even a rinky-dink wedding gig in"—he sighed in disgust—"Cow-Pie, Pennsylvania."

Something in Dad's voice made me wish that I was riding out with him, or that I could pay him for my lessons so he didn't have to worry about money— or that I could at least find the right words to cheer him up. "Well," I said, pausing to think. "Do you at least get a little wedding cake?"

That got me a chuckle. "I like a girl with her priorities in order," Dad said. "How about this? I'll snag *you* a piece if I can. Anyway, kid, I've got to watch the road. Give Ella a big honkin' smooch on the nose for me, would you?"

I was still upset when I hung up the phone, but it was hard to stay mad at Dad. He'd sounded tired and lonely, like he was heading all that way just to play in a big, empty room.

When I returned to the living room, I found Momma sitting on the couch with her back to me. "Are you all right?" she asked. Her voice didn't match the question at all—her words came out as dark as coal.

"I'm okay," I replied, though that wasn't all-the-way true. "A gig came up and Dad really had to take it."

"That's what he does best," Momma said. "Why would I expect anything different?"

I wasn't even sure if she was talking to me anymore. What I did know was that between Dad's disappearing and Momma's turning into a black cloud, I just wanted to go to my room and lie down for a long nap.

Then Ella's tongue smacked me on the palm of my hand. I looked down and saw her staring up beside me. She kept licking my hand, her eyes locked on me—and I knew that giving up on the rest of the day simply wasn't an option.

I knelt down and hugged Ella around the neck. "I bet I know what you'd like to do," I told her.

"Ready, pups?" Ricky said, shaking a knotted rope toy. "Go-go-go!" He hurled the rope across the length of his backyard, and Ella and Hamlet dashed after it. Well, it was more like Ella dashed and Hamlet lumbered. I couldn't believe how big Ham had gotten. Back in July, he'd just been a little heap of wrinkly skin—and now, only three months later, he was already bigger than Ella.

And he was stronger than her, too. I had to laugh as they played tug-of-war with the rope. Hamlet stood there like an anchor while Ella yanked on the other end without any luck.

"Look at those two," Ricky commented. "Crazy and Lazy."

"Is that fun for him?" I asked.

"Pretty sure," Ricky replied. "He plays the same way with me. He brings me the rope and then makes me do all the work."

"Sounds kind of smart when you put it that way," I said.

We watched the dogs struggle over their toy. A gust of wind swirled the fallen leaves on the ground, and I zipped my jacket up to my neck.

After a minute, Ricky glanced over and spoke. "He's really missed her, you know."

"Really?" I asked.

"Well, yeah," he replied, shoving his hands into the pouch of his hoodie. "It's been about a hundred years since you came over."

I rolled my eyes and grinned. That was Ricky-speak for anything that took longer than he wanted. "It hasn't been that long."

"It's been a whole month," Ricky said. "Ham was getting worried."

"I don't think he worries much about anything," I said. Ham was sitting in the middle of the yard, gripping the rope in his teeth as Ella tugged away at the other end.

"Fine," Ricky sighed. "I was worried."

I turned in surprise. "About what?"

Ricky frowned and stepped ahead of me. "All right, guys!" he called out to our pups. "Bring it here; I'll throw it again!"

Ella and Hamlet didn't even look at him.

"Why were you worried?" I asked again.

Ricky turned sharply. "Because you made a new best friend and forgot all about us!"

I had to stare at him for a moment. "He's not my best friend," I cried. "He's my dad!"

Ricky squinted. "What do you mean, your dad?" he asked. "I'm talking about Darla."

A laugh sputtered out of me before I could catch it. "Darla Washington?" I asked.

"It's not funny," he murmured.

"Darla's not my new best friend," I said.

"Could have fooled me," he replied. "You're always hanging out with her anymore."

"Because of Talent Pool," I told him.

"Just forget it," Ricky said. He headed toward our dogs, but I grabbed onto his arm.

"Wait," I said. "Did you really think I didn't want to be friends anymore?"

He looked down at one of his sneakers.

"I could help you with that musical if you want," he offered. He reached into his hoodie pouch and pulled out a pair of drumsticks, which he always seemed to be carrying ever since he'd joined band. "Like, you could come over here to practice the songs. And I could be your official beat keeper."

"You don't have to do that," I said. "How about I just do a better job at hanging out?"

He hesitated. "…Yeah?"

"Come on, Ricky," I said. "Darla's all right, but I only have one best friend."

He took a deep breath and as he let it out, his lips spread into a smile. "Your songs sound funny," he said. "I've heard you guys practicing."

"Thanks," I replied, tightening my cheeks to pinch my grin back.

"What's the one Darla's always mumbling?"

"The hamster song?"

"Yeah," Ricky said, "do that one!"

I rolled my eyes, but I was actually glad he asked. "Count me in, beat keeper," I said. Ricky patted a drumstick against his leg as I tapped my foot. Then I sang:

"*H-A-M-S-T-E-R,*
Riding in my hamster ball.

Cereals are what we eat.
Grains and nuts, they can't be beat."

Then I began to punch the air in front of me in time with the song. "*Gottaeat'em, gottaeat'em, gottaeat'em, gottaeat'em…*"

We both broke up in giggles. "I can't believe Billy Cutler's going to sing that," he said. Billy was a fifth grader who always wore dress shirts and suspenders to school.

"He's pretty good," I replied. "You'll see."

"Hey," Ricky said, "I have a music trick. Want to see it?"

I nodded in agreement. Ricky raised his drumsticks above his head and clicked them together four times. "One, two, three, four!"

Immediately, Hamlet dropped his end of the rope and strolled toward us. Ella hurried along with him, whipping the rope against her side, running circles around the big dog as they approached.

"When'd you teach him that?" I asked, impressed.

Ricky shrugged. "About…ninety-nine years ago," he said, rubbing the crease of Hamlet's brow. "Let's go in and get them a treat."

Ricky clicked his drumsticks and Hamlet followed him to the sliding door. I hooked on Ella's leash and brought her along.

As we entered the kitchen, Ricky shouted out, "Mom, where are those sweet potato thingies?"

"Whoa, whoa!" Mr. Jenkins said. He was standing at the counter with a slow cooker lid in one hand and a big spoon in the other. "How about an inside voice, bud?"

"Sorry, Dad," Ricky said. "Are you sneaking into Mom's chili?"

Mr. Jenkins quickly wiped his mouth with the back of his hand. "You'd never prove it in a court of law," he said, and I had to grin. "Latasha, has my son invited you to dinner yet?"

I really wanted to stay. In that moment, I wanted nothing more than to be part of Ricky's family—his just-right family where Mom never looked mean, the worst thing Dad did was sneak a bite of dinner early, and nobody ever got forgotten. I wanted that, even if it was just for a meal.

But I wasn't a Jenkins. I was a Gandy.

"I can't," I replied, the words more bitter than coffee. "I promised Momma I'd cook."

I trudged up the stairs to our apartment with Ella at my heels. I couldn't think of a single thing I wanted to do less than make a meatball hoagie dinner right now—but that had been the plan, and Dad's skipping out didn't change that.

I opened the door to find Momma already in the kitchen. She was listening on the phone. "See you in forty-five," she said, and then she hung up.

"Who was that?" I asked flatly.

"Pizza Franco," Momma said. That perked me up—Pizza Franco is my favorite restaurant in the whole city. "I thought you might not feel like cooking tonight."

I was so grateful it made my knees weak. "Thanks, Momma."

She took Ella's leash from my hands and unhooked her for me. "Can we talk for a second?" she asked as Ella darted off to the living room.

I dropped into a chair at the table and Momma stood in front of me.

"I owe you an apology," she said. "For earlier."

My brow crinkled. "Momma—"

"—Hang on, I want to be honest with you," she told me. "No secrets, right?"

I nodded.

"When your father called…" she said, halting. She sat beside me and started over. "Before you were born—when you were a baby—your father pulled that disappearing act a lot. Even when I really needed him here. Especially then."

I finally had to ask her. "Is that why you split up?"

"There wasn't just one thing," Momma replied. "But…it mattered. It made me feel like I was nothing."

I knew exactly what she meant.

"When he did that to you today," Momma continued, "all I could think about was how lousy that used to make me feel. But I shouldn't have been hung up on me. I should have been there for you. I'm sorry for not being right there, sweetie."

I bolted to my feet and clasped Momma in the tightest hug I'd ever given. Today might not have been the perfect day I'd planned, but she had rescued it from being a disaster.

Once I unwrapped myself from Momma, she stood up. "I hope you got that pup plenty of exercise," she said. "I ordered her a Franco's frosted cupcake for her anniversary."

As Momma gathered dishes for dinner, I remembered the talk I'd had with Ricky—how I'd been hurting his feelings without even knowing it. "Maybe if I sat Dad down and really talked to him," I said, "he'd be different."

Momma gave me a sympathetic smile. "You've got a good heart," she said.

I hate when Momma says things like that—things that sound like compliments but really mean, *Silly girl.* "I trained Ella to be nice to Hamlet," I insisted.

"Training dogs is hard work," Momma agreed. "But training people is harder."

Chapter Eight
The Lonely Dog Blues

I quickly learned that there is one major difference between teaching something to Ella and teaching something to Dad: Ella is always around to learn from me. The longer I waited, the less sure I became. What if I told him how I felt and he got mad at me? That was another difference between him and my pup—if my dad didn't like what I had to say, he could just pack up his keyboard and leave.

Or, even worse, what if I told him how he'd hurt me and he just didn't care?

That was my main worry as I waited for Dad to trudge up our front stairs. Well, that and Momma. She was standing with me in the kitchen and her arms were crossed so tight that her muscles showed, like that time in second grade when I'd painted Ella's toenails and let her run around before they'd dried. I'd waited another two weeks for Dad to come back around—I prayed that Momma wouldn't scare him right out the door. I reached down and gave my whirling pup a squeeze on the neck for courage. At least I knew how Ella would react. She was already bouncing in excitement.

I opened our door and when I saw my father, I had to smile. One of his hands gripped the underside of his keyboard, and the other held a bulging bouquet of flowers. He offered the bunch to me, its pink and white and yellow and red blooms bright enough to burst. "Hey, kid."

I clasped the bundled stems and turned to show them off. "Momma, *look*!"

Momma smiled at me, then shifted her eyes to Dad. "Glad you decided to come out of hiding," she said.

I wanted to throw her a smirk, but first I had to

raise my bouquet out of Ella's curious reach.

"Are these lilies?" I asked my dad. I'd been helping Mrs. Okocho tend to her garden for the last few weeks to earn money for Christmas presents—she was turning me into a regular flower expert.

"Good eye," he replied. "And they're just for you."

"None for Momma?" I asked, glancing back at her stern face.

"Well…" he said, "I've got something else for her."

He set his keyboard on the kitchen table and unslung its stand from his shoulder. "Down, girl!" I hissed as Ella put her paws up and nosed at the keys.

"She's okay," Dad said, and he pulled an envelope from inside his leather jacket. I watched Momma's face soften as he walked it over to her. Dad spoke quietly, so I had to strain to hear him over Ella's ruckus.

"It's less than all I owe," he told her. "But it's my absolute best."

"Patrick," Momma replied, her voice warmer than I'd heard in weeks. She took the envelope like she was afraid of breaking it. "What's this about?"

"I got some news today," Dad said. He turned to face the both of us. "I have been ordained!"

I felt like I knew that word, but it couldn't possibly mean what I thought. "You became a priest?" I asked.

"To be more exact," Dad replied, "I became a Minister. The bandleader called me up last night. Asked if I wanted to make things official and join his crew full-time."

Dad and I flashed our matching smiles. "That's awesome!" I cried.

"Good for you," Momma added, and I could tell she really meant it.

Even Ella got into the act, circling Dad's feet and poking at his knees for attention. "Don't you worry," he told her. "I didn't forget you." He reached into another pocket and removed a chew bone for Ella.

I watched him hand the toy to my girl and I had to wonder: how could someone be so thoughtless part of the time, and get things exactly right other times?

Ella seized the toy in her teeth and sprinted off to the living room with it. Then she dashed into my room. Then Momma's.

"Ella!" she grumbled.

My pup skittered back into the kitchen, wagging wildly, and darted out again. *Sorry, Mrs. Okocho*, I thought.

Momma sighed and took the flowers from me. "How about I get these in some water for you?"

"Thanks," I said. Then I remembered something

I'd learned while helping in the garden. "Oh, and cut the stems on a slant. They'll last longer."

Momma pursed her lips at me before she left the room.

"Well, it's true, you know," I muttered.

Ella bounded into the room a third time, whipping her head around with the bone between her jaws.

"Boy, oh, boy," Dad mused. "Does she get like that a lot?"

"You have no idea," I said, looking at the linoleum.

Dad chuckled as she dashed out again. "All right, that's it," he announced. "We'll never get any practicing done with her like that. How about we settle Miss Ella down with a nice, long walk?"

"You can let her snuffle around a little, but keep her walking," I explained. "She has to know you're in charge."

"Am I, now?" Dad commented. He jingled Ella's collar. "You heard it. Let's go!"

Ella stopped sniffing the bushes and we continued slowly toward Friendship Park. I hadn't taken Ella there in a while, and she seemed even more curious than usual about every sight and smell.

I stole a glance at my father as we walked. Dad's good news had been really exciting, but it hadn't been enough to make me forget last month. I had to say something.

"Daddy," I began timidly. "We need to talk about something."

"Uh-oh," he replied.

I felt my insides begin to tingle. "Uh-oh, what?" I asked.

"Conversations that start that way are never about good things," Dad said. "It's never like, 'We need to talk…about how great you are!' It's always bad news." Then he glanced at me with that sly grin of his. "Or is it?"

"It's…" I wanted to go on, but the words seemed to be stuck beneath my collarbone. Finally, I burst out, "We need to borrow your keyboard."

"My keyboard?" he asked.

"For the Innovation Conversation," I added. "Darla only has an upright piano at home. We need something for her to play at the competition."

"Is that so?"

I nodded insistently. It wasn't what I'd really wanted to talk about, but it wasn't a lie, either. Actually, Darla had been hounding me about it ever since I'd mentioned that my dad played the keyboard. She did it in her usual Darla way—by showing everyone her clipboard with our supplies list, and mentioning how "the keyboard is *not* crossed off yet, Latasha!"

Dad shrugged. "I have a second keyboard at my place," he said. "From my early days. It's only a sixty-one key, and, honestly, its carrying bag is fancier than the board itself. But it sounds fine. You can borrow it for as long as you need."

I smiled and hugged his arm.

We reached the loop of road that circled Friendship Park. Dad stopped at the corner as we took it all in. A few runners in sweats were jogging on the sidewalk, while a couple of little kids played Tag near the drinking fountain.

"Now, before we go and have a grand old time," Dad said, "how about you tell me what's really on your mind?"

I eyed him nervously. "What do you mean?"

Dad cocked his head. "Kid, I might not be Dad of the Year, but I've got eyes and ears." He choked up on Ella's leash to keep her on the sidewalk. "It's all right, really. Untrouble your brain."

I'd thought it would be tough to have a serious talk with a puppy wiggling between our shins—but once I started in, I barely noticed the distraction. I told Dad about how I'd waited for him, and how I'd gone from angry, to worried, to embarrassed and back. "And then you called, but it was like you almost forgot," I went on. "And Momma was super mad… and I felt like you didn't care about me at all."

Dad shook his head. "That's not true," he replied. "That's never been true."

"It's how you made me feel." I watched some cars pass as I worked up the courage to finish. "You can't go away without warning me," I told him. "You can't forget me. You can't."

My father watched me silently.

I couldn't stand the quiet. "Are you mad?" I asked.

Dad rubbed at a spot near his eye. "I'm proud," he said. "That was brave of you to tell me all that. And I promise—I won't forget you."

And then he took his hat off and fitted it on my head. I touched the brim and felt so relieved that I probably could have taken a nap right there on the corner.

"That's a loan," he said with a wink. "Now, what say we go and run your girl's battery out?"

I looked down, and when I saw Ella I had to hold back a laugh. "Daddy?" I pointed to the panting pup.

It seemed that Ella had felt like having a nap herself. While Dad and I were talking, she'd circled him twice, wrapping the leash around his ankles, and

then laid down to rest. "Ella," I called, almost singing. The pup looked at me, but just huffed and shifted her head to a more comfortable position.

Dad tried to lift his foot out of the tangle, but he couldn't wriggle free. "How about that?" he said. "She trapped me."

After our talk, Dad really did do better. He was still kind of late, but he came by to hang out every day he had a rehearsal. We talked about the latest news in our lives, like the new (old) band Dad had discovered at the record store, and the "weird lunch" contest I'd judged at our table at school. (For the record, Ricky gulped down a dozen deviled eggs and had to go to the nurse's office for the afternoon, but Dante won by making a Cheetos-and-Little-Debbies sandwich. And I *lost* by having to watch him eat it!)

Other times, we just traded complaints about the folks who were on our backs. For me, it was Miss Prooper, because I hadn't followed every single one of her silly instructions for our homework—as if it mattered whether I drew my map of the United States in purple pencil instead of black. For Dad, it was his bandleader, Joe—"For no reason at all!" he'd say.

The rest of our time together, my father worked with me to finish "The Lonely Dog Blues." He helped me find a good key to create a simple tune for Darla to play. After that, I just had to practice and practice until the song felt perfect. By mid-November, it seemed really close. But I had this pesky feeling that things could be a *little* better.

"No nerves allowed," Dad told me. "It's just you, me, and Sleepy McGee over there."

He meant Ella. We'd walked her before starting, so she was sprawled out on the couch, tongue almost to the floor. Momma had gone downstairs to play cards with Mrs. Okocho, so Dad and I had set up the keyboard he'd lent me in the living room.

"Here we go," Dad said. He played my song's little intro, and I began to sing:

"If you want to stay smiling,
Then don't you look at me.
I'm the saddest little puppy
That you ever did see.
You heard the news?
I've got the lonely dog blues.
What will I do?
I've got the lonely dog blues.
Clock tells me it's been an hour
Feels like it's been a year

Where, oh where, did my owner go,
And when will she come back here?
I'm chewing shoes.
I've got the lonely dog blues.
It's such a snooze.
I've got the lonely dog blues."

I stopped singing and looked at my father. He kept playing the song's twelve-bar progression, his eyes closed. "Dad?" I asked.

He opened his eyes and smiled at me. "You're good, kid," he said, resting his hands in his lap. "I really like it."

"That's it," I said with a smirk. "You really like it."

That's all any adult I'd sung for could tell me. Mr. Harvey, Mr. and Mrs. Jenkins, Darla's grandmother, Momma—no one had had a single comment for me except, "It's great! It's funny! It's wonderful!" The only one who'd had any suggestion at all was Mrs. Okocho—and her big contribution was, "You should bark like a dog after every verse." I needed advice— real advice.

"Well…" Dad said slowly. "There are a couple little places you could work on."

I swiftly flipped to a clean page in my notebook. "Now that's more like it!" I exclaimed, crossing to sit beside my pup. "What's off?"

"The first line," Dad replied. "I'm not feeling the rhythm of it. Is there a way you can change it so it matches the third line?"

I repeated those lines in my head. He was right—they were different. One had more syllables than the other. "What about…*If you want to keep your smile…*"

Dad clapped his hands together so loudly that it startled Ella awake. "Yes!" he said.

I scribbled down the change. "What else?" I asked.

"That bit about having the lonely dog blues is cute," he said, "but it needs to get bigger by the end. Like—" He played the last few chords and sang for me:

"*It's such a snooze.*
I've got the lonely dog blues.
I've got the left-me-all-alone-ly, all-locked-inside-my-home-ly dog blues!"

I added that note, too. I couldn't just copy his new line word for word—we had to write all the lyrics ourselves—but maybe I'd be able to use the general idea. "Thanks, Daddy," I said.

"Outside of that, I love it," he told me, standing up from the chair we'd dragged out of my room. He moved to the couch and plopped down with an arm around me. "If you guys don't win, the judges are crazy."

I hugged my notebook to my chest.

"I think we can wrap for today," he said. "Let's pack up."

I grabbed the keyboard's carrying bag. It was made from this shimmery nylon, and it had special lettering stitched on the side, like on Ricky's custom Steelers jacket. I ran my thumb across the letters— *The Kidd on Keys*.

"Daddy?"

"Yeah?"

I swallowed to keep my throat from going dry. "Do you absolutely have to go down to Florida for Thanksgiving?"

I felt him sigh next to me. "She *is* my mum," he replied. "I ought to see her once a year."

"I know," I replied. "It's just—couldn't she come up here instead?"

Dad shook his head. "We've talked about this before." He lifted his arm off me and stood again to stretch.

I knew Dad didn't much like the idea, but my friends and I had all been talking about Thanksgiving at lunch and it had gotten me thinking. The Jenkinses had plans to visit Ricky's grandparents and all of his cousins near Detroit. Darla and her grandma were having a big potluck with some families in their apartment building. And all I had was a little dinner with Momma and Mrs. Okocho. The only kid having a lamer Thanksgiving than me was Dante—and he said he was happy about it because he liked eating Boston Market better than turkey anyway.

But I couldn't just pretend like I was satisfied. "There's plenty of room," I insisted. "And I promise, Momma will do all the cooking. I won't let Mrs. Okocho make anything."

That at least made Dad grin a little. "Mum already got me a ticket down," he said.

I smirked—but not for long. "How about Christmas, then?" I suggested. "She could come up, and so could your stepdad."

"Jeez, Latasha," he moaned, "can we just drop it?" His voice felt like a jab with a long needle.

Dad must have seen the tears on their way. "I'm sorry, kid," he said. "It's not because of you."

"Then what is it?" I asked.

Dad knelt down to my eye level. "Do you remember that thing I told you about my mum?" he asked gently. "About how she can shrink you down with her words?"

I nodded.

He reached out and rubbed my shoulder. "I don't want her to come up here," he said, "and shrink what you and I have."

I guessed that was supposed to cheer me up, because Dad stood again and exhaled in satisfaction. "So," he said brightly, "let's just forget about her, and stick to having fun, huh?"

If only it was that easy.

At every Thanksgiving dinner, we have this little tradition where we hold hands and list a few things from the past year that we appreciate. It's Momma's version of saying grace.

We sat at one end of Mrs. Okocho's table—Momma at the head, Mrs. O to the left, me to the right. Mrs. Okocho went first, saying how she was thankful for how Momma and I had welcomed her into our lives, and a bunch of other nice stuff that normally would have made me feel all happy and full and loved. But I wasn't listening all that closely. I wasn't watching her, or Momma, or even the big spread of turkey and mashed potatoes and buttery rolls. My eyes kept drifting to the other end of the table, and all I could see was how much room we had left down there. And it made me want to hide in my bed, tucked safely under the covers like the way I'd left Ella before coming downstairs.

"Latasha," Momma said, squeezing my hand. I glanced over and forced out a smile. "Your turn, sweetie."

I realized that I'd missed what Momma had said altogether. "I'm…" I began, looking over the table. "I'm grateful for our dinner. And for Ella being okay. And—" I narrowed my eyes. "And I hope Daddy is having just as good of a Thanksgiving as I am."

I wasn't even sure what that meant, but it must have been good enough to fool everybody, because Momma smiled and we all let go of each other's hands. "All right," Mrs. Okocho said. "Let us feast!"

As she cut the turkey, I stole another glance at the foot of the table, and I gripped the edge of the tablecloth until my fingernails went pale.

Chapter Nine

Secret Weapon

On the Monday after Thanksgiving, my father called to check on me and share stories from his trip. "Three days of lectures," Dad griped. "'*When are you going to settle down? When will you get a* real *job? And take off that hat at the table!*'"

I doubted that my grandma really sounded like the Wicked Witch of the West, but Dad's impression made my frustration with him melt away.

"I'm a hat guy, what can I say?" he went on. "Not my fault I got this giant-sized noggin."

I giggled. "Your head's not that big."

"It's probably from all the brains up in there," Dad said. "Jokes aside, though, how about we do something together? You pick what it is."

I squeezed the phone in excitement. "Can it be anything?"

"Not anything," he replied. "It can't be inside the apartment. We have to go somewhere."

That was fine—I already had something in mind. "I want you to meet my friend, Ricky," I said. "And his family."

"Ehh…"

"It's our school's winter concert next week," I explained. "Momma's coming with me. Ricky's playing these huge drums—they're practically bigger than him!"

"Timpani?" he asked.

"That's the name!" I replied. "Will you come? You can have the aisle seat if you want."

"Okay, okay," Dad gave in with a chuckle. "It's a date."

"I wanted a clip-on," Ricky said, tugging on his necktie, "but Mom did *this* to me."

Momma smiled at him. "You look very dapper, Ricky," she said.

He just blinked at us. I leaned over and stated, "It's a compliment."

"Oh—thanks!" Ricky said. "Is your dad still coming?"

I patted the empty aisle seat next to me. "Any second," I replied.

"Cool," Ricky said. "I've got to get back to the band room. See you after!"

My eyes followed him as he ran past the few rows behind us and out the back of the auditorium. When I resettled in my seat, I noticed Momma watching me.

"I'm not worried," I told her.

"Good," she said. "There's still time yet."

It was 7:20 in the evening, which gave Dad ten minutes before he was officially late. I really wasn't bothered, though—it wouldn't even be so bad if he came in a minute or two behind. The chorus performed before the band anyway. And besides, it was the part that came after the concert that mattered most. I decided that I wouldn't look back again until he arrived.

To kill some time, I studied the stage for a moment and then shut my eyes and tried to recall every detail about it. The stage's curtain, a heavy, dark purple drape, was closed. Some risers were set up in front of it for the chorus. An upright piano stood off to the side. I knew it came from the band room, which is where we'd been having our rehearsals for the Innovation Conversation. It was for the chorus's accompanist—which is a fancy name for "piano player" that Darla insists I use on her.

I felt a tap on my shoulder. "Can I sit here?" said a voice.

I opened my eyes. It wasn't Dad—it was Dante.

"I'm holding it," I replied.

"Oh," he said with a frown.

"There's space on this end," Momma offered, pointing a thumb to her far side. "Here—I'll slide down one so you kids can talk."

I didn't really have anything to say to Dante, but Momma grabbed her coat and shifted over a seat anyway. "Sorry," Dante mumbled, stepping on my shoes as he crowded past me.

Momma smiled at Dante as he sat. "So, too cool to sit with your family?" she asked him.

Dante shrugged. "They had important stuff to do. They're picking me up after." He turned to me. "I just wanted to see Jenkins bang on those big old Tiffany drums."

"*Timpani*," I replied.

"What. Ever," Dante scoffed. "I heard he's got to stand on a ladder to play them, *heh-heh*."

I rolled my eyes. Outside, a bell sounded, and then the auditorium lights flashed a few times. A flood of families hurried in from the hallway to take their seats. I draped my coat across the one I was holding for Dad.

A minute later, the chorus filed out onto the risers. Then the lights went down and our principal,

Dr. DeSoto, came onstage to introduce the chorus director.

I sighed and wished Dante hadn't worked his way in between Momma and me. I could have used an arm to clutch onto.

Then I heard him next to me. "Mind if I join you?"

My whole face lit up with a smile—but Dante leaned over before I could speak. "Actually," he said, "it's *reserved*."

"Can it," I whispered. "This is my dad!"

Dad tipped his hat.

"Sorry, sir," Dante replied.

"Sir…" Dad repeated with a chuckle. He handed my coat back to me and ducked into his seat. "Sorry I'm running behind."

The audience applauded as Dr. DeSoto finished speaking. "You're just in time," I said.

"If I'm late to practice," Dad told me, "the bandleader fines me twenty-five bucks. But if he wants to run practice late—well, that's all fine and dandy."

I peeked over at Dad. "Does he really fine you if you're late?" I asked.

Dad shot me a *you'd-better-believe-it* glance.

On stage, the director gave a signal to his

accompanist. The piano sounded out and the chorus began to sing. It was different from our choir at church—a lot of the chorus kids stood kind of stiffly as they sang—but they still sounded good.

Dad was having fun, too. Through every song, he shimmied in his chair and tapped his feet to the beat. When the chorus wrapped up with "Jingle Bell Rock," I even caught him playing along with the accompanist on an imaginary keyboard in his lap.

As the chorus director guided his kids out a side door, Dad leaned toward me. "Thanks for inviting me," he said in my ear.

"Sure, Dad," I replied, trying to sound calm and not like I was so happy I could squeal.

"Were any of those kids in your Gifted and Talented club?" he asked.

"A few," I replied. "I'll introduce you to them during cookie time."

"Cookie time?"

"Yeah!" I said. "After the show, everyone's invited to the cafeteria for cocoa and these huge oatmeal cookies."

Dad scratched his chin with his thumb and gave a big nod.

"They're from the PTA," I explained. "Here's my plan. I'll get cookies for all three of us, and Momma can introduce you to the other grown-ups."

"Got it all figured out, huh?" he said, still watching the stage. Two custodians were up there, moving the last riser out of the way. When they finished, the purple curtain opened to reveal the school band. They were still finding their seats and fixing their music stands.

"Look, look!" Dante whispered to me.

At the back of the stage, we could see Ricky stepping in behind the timpani, which looked like two huge, shiny witch's cauldrons on wheels. He practically disappeared behind them, until he stood up on a stool. Dante couldn't stop snickering.

After another introduction from Dr. DeSoto, the band began to play. To be honest, they weren't as good as the chorus. All of their songs were slowed down to make them easier to play, so "Good King Wenceslas" felt like it was half an hour long. Then, on the next tune, the clarinets kept making weird squeaks as they played. At least Ricky sounded good. He was right on the beat with the timpani. And loud, too. I decided that's what I would say if Ricky asked how I liked the concert: *You were super easy to hear!*

But about halfway through the performance, something wonderful happened. My dad slipped his hand around mine and held it tightly. And he didn't let go. From then on, nothing on stage really mattered at all.

The band finished their last song and everyone applauded. Dad let go of my hand so we could join in. We all stood and I clapped hard—I was happy for my friend, but even more, I was excited about cookie time!

As the applause died out, Dad hugged me with

one arm. Then he told me, "I have to go."

I stared up at him.

He looked over at Momma. "Steph, I'm sorry, I've got to skip out."

"You okay?" she asked.

I tugged at his sleeve. "Daddy," I said quietly, "what's wrong? What'd I do?"

"It's not you, kid," he replied. Dad sniffled and then grabbed his nose with his thumb and forefinger. "We'll talk soon, okay? Promise."

I watched him push past the crowd in the aisle, holding his nose like he'd smelled something awful, and I just wanted to scream after him. How could he not understand how much this meant to me?

After a minute, Momma led us out to the hallway. "Let's go home," I said to her.

"I know, sweetie," she replied. "But we should find Ricky and say something nice first."

We went to the cafeteria. Inside, all of the kids were meeting up with their families for snacks. I had to blink my eyes for a second—the last thing I wanted was for anybody to see me cry.

We spotted a table where Ricky was laughing with his parents. "Hi, Latasha!" Mrs. Jenkins said with a wave.

Ricky looked around us. "Hey," he said, "your dad

didn't make it?"

"No, he came," I said, my voice quaking. "He had to go."

Dante stepped up next to me. "I saw him," he added. "She's not lying."

"Why would I lie?" I snapped at him.

Momma put a hand on my back to calm me down. "You sounded great," she told Ricky.

He beamed at us. "Yeah, I was pretty loud, huh?"

A few days later, I found myself staring at Ricky's timpani in the band room. We'd just finished another rehearsal for Talent Pool and I could hear the other kids gathering their things behind me. "And next time," Darla warned one of them, "you'd better know all the words to 'Pesky Pete the Parakeet'!"

"Let's cool off, Darla," Mr. Harvey said. "We've still got nine days and another rehearsal yet. Everyone is doing great work."

I wasn't so sure about that. Practice hadn't gone well today. I guess you could say that we sounded less like the chorus had and more like the band. We had a lot of work to do and not much time—but right then, I wasn't really worrying about it. I had other thoughts on my mind.

"Can I help you with that?" asked Mr. Harvey.

I turned and saw that everyone else was gone. Mr. Harvey pointed to Dad's keyboard. I'd been zipping it up in its bag before I got distracted.

I decided to just ask what I'd been wondering. "Mr. Harvey," I began, "how do you teach somebody who doesn't want to learn?"

"I think you and Darla are being a little hard on Gautam," he said. "'Pesky Pete' is a tricky song."

"I don't mean Gautam," I replied. "I just mean… anybody."

Mr. Harvey took a knee on one of the chairs across from me. "Having trouble with a friend?" he asked.

Just then, I thought of Dad's big, shoulder-shaking laugh. I zipped the case shut. "Sort of, yeah."

He studied my face for a second. "Do you want to talk about it?"

I shook my head and stood up. "Mrs. Okocho's waiting for me," I replied.

Mr. Harvey lifted the keyboard bag by its strap. "Gosh!" he said, tilting like the bag weighed a hundred pounds. "You carried this yourself? You are strong!"

"I just want to know really fast," I said. "What do

you do if someone doesn't want to learn?"

Mr. Harvey led me out of the band room. "You know," he replied, "I've never met a student who doesn't *want* to learn—only students who don't *believe* that they can. Does that make sense?"

"You mean like they don't believe in themselves?"

"Right."

We walked together down the empty hall. "So how do you fix that?" I asked.

"I can't tell you how many times I've asked myself that question," Mr. Harvey replied. "The trouble is, you or I can't force somebody to learn."

I let out a long breath as we pushed open the school's front doors.

"But here's what we can do," Mr. Harvey told me. "We can care. We can listen. And we can try to understand."

As soon as Mrs. Okocho got us home—and as soon as I could get Ella to stop hopping all over me—I grabbed our phone and called Dad's cell. After a few rings he picked up. "Hey there, kid," he said. "What's the buzz?"

"Can we talk for a minute?" I asked.

Suddenly, his voice sounded far away, like he was holding the phone away from his mouth. "Two minutes! It's my daughter," Dad said. "Joe, Joe, I know."

I winced. He must have been at band practice.

"Yeah, yeah, twenty-dollar fine, I'm shocked," I heard him say. Then Dad's voice got clearer to me. "Sorry, my dear. Everything okay?"

"Did I get you in trouble?" I asked.

"No, it's my fault," he said. "I left my ringer on. But it's actually great that you called."

"It is?"

"Yes, indeedy," he replied. "This Saturday, keep your schedule clear. We've got some very important business."

Dad didn't explain what our "important business" was—but it must have been a pretty big deal, because on Saturday, he pulled up outside our house exactly on time.

"Hustle! Hustle!" Dad said as I climbed into his station wagon. "We don't want to be late."

"Sorry," I said, fixing my second mitten. "When you said noon, I thought you meant more like…

Dad-noon."

He grinned at me. "Not today, kid," he said. "We've got an appointment to make."

"Where are we going?" I asked.

Dad started the car's engine. "You'll see. Wave to Ella."

I looked toward the house. Up in our apartment, Ella had pushed the living room curtains aside and put her paws on the windowsill. I waved to her as we rode away, and she wiggled back at me.

We reached the corner and turned onto Penn Avenue. Dad's car rumbled past the dollar store and the cemetery, and then we hit the stoplight by Children's Hospital.

"How cool is it that your mother works there?" asked Dad.

"Pretty cool," I replied.

"You should be proud of her," he said.

"Well, yeah, I am," I said—like I needed to be told! The light turned green and we moved on.

We passed by the 31st Street Bridge and then slowed to a crawl in the Strip District among the packs of Saturday shoppers who were lined up for their fresh breads and seafood and vegetables. As we waited for the van ahead of us to parallel park, Dad turned to me.

"I owe you an explanation," he said. "About the band concert."

I was relieved that I didn't have to bring it up. "What happened?" I asked.

"I…" he said with a frown. "I got a nosebleed."

I instantly remembered the last time he'd gotten one. "Are you still hurt from Ella?"

"No, no," he assured me. "I just get them sometimes. When I'm really nervous."

I squinted at him, trying to imagine my dad being nervous about anything. I couldn't picture it.

He drummed on the steering wheel with his palms. "It was the crowd, I guess," he said.

"You play for crowds all the time," I replied.

"I mean all those other parents," he said. "I kept thinking about meeting them, you know? Playing it in my head. I don't know any of them. What were we going to talk about? What would I say?"

"I don't know," I said. "How about, 'Hi, I'm Latasha's dad. When I was in school, I was in band, too. And now I have a career as a musician extraordinaire.'"

Dad glanced at me with a little smile. "You know what I like about you?" he asked.

"What?"

"When you look at me," he said, "you see a

different story than most people do."

We finally got past the Strip and into downtown Pittsburgh. We turned onto a side street and found a parking meter. "Can you at least give me a hint about where we're going?" I begged as we got out.

Dad fed the meter some quarters. "I'm going to show you my secret weapon," he said.

I stared at my father—he could be so weird sometimes!

"Let's march," he commanded, and we tramped down the block.

"What secret weapon?" I asked as we cut through the cold.

He looked at me and said, "Against feeling nervous."

Dad stopped us outside a building with a pair of spotless white doors and a brass doorbell beside them. A man's name was printed in big lettering on the doorframe. I couldn't tell if it was a store, or what.

"Ever been here before?" he asked.

I shook my head.

"Me neither." And with that, Dad rang the doorbell. A thin man with a gray mustache answered.

"Good afternoon," Dad said. "I'm Mr. Kidd. I have a twelve-thirty appointment."

"Please!" the man said, and he opened the door

wide for us.

Inside, it looked like a cross between a Macy's and a mansion. The walls were lined with displays of suits, shirts, and ties, but the floor was all dark brown hardwood, and scattered about were wooden chairs with fancy carvings and silky cushions. Right in the center of the room, a big chandelier hung from the ceiling.

"Will we be taking measurements today?" asked the man with the mustache. I realized he must be a tailor.

"Nope, I'm easy," Dad replied, unbuttoning his peacoat. "An off-the-rack kind of fellow. Let's pick out some options, and my lovely daughter here will help me make a final choice."

My cheeks got cherry-hot. "May I take your coat?" asked the tailor.

"Thank you," I replied. I stuffed my mittens in my pockets and handed it over.

The tailor went off with our jackets, leaving us alone in the showroom.

"So, we're going suit shopping?" I asked.

"What can I say? I love the way new clothes feel," Dad explained. "This is what I do when I need to feel better. When I'm nervous, feeling shrunk down…or working with a jerk…"

"You mean Joe?" I asked.

Dad held his hands up. "Hey, you said it, not me!"

I shot my father a playful sneer. The tailor returned. "Young lady," he said, "why don't you have a seat? Your father and I will go find some good fits, and I'll send him out to you."

I eased into one of the fancy chairs. The thing was more comfortable than my bed! And then I waited and thought about why we were here. I'd never seen Dad wear a suit before. How could he even afford to shop at a place like this?

I was able to wonder about all of that and then hum my way through "The Lonely Dog Blues" three whole times before Dad came back.

But when he returned, he looked like a totally different guy. Dad's hat was gone, his hair was pulled back, and he'd changed into a sharp navy blue suit with a striped pattern. His tie was red with tiny white diamond shapes, and a handkerchief peeked out of his pocket. His shoes were as shiny as black ice.

"So tell me," he said, "what do I look like?"

"Well…" I began. "You look great! But—kind of like a banker."

Dad stretched his arms so his cufflinks showed. "You think?"

"Yeah, definitely," I said. "A banker with a huge

office…with, like, an aquarium in it."

"All right, I get it," he laughed. "It's not quite right. Back in a few!"

I waited a little while longer, and then Dad returned with a brand-new look. This time, he had a brown sport coat and a stiff black dress shirt.

I shook my head. "Now you look like a professor," I said. "Who teaches…German, or something."

Dad straightened his back. "Vat makes you say zat?" he demanded.

He modeled a half-dozen more suits for me after that. Each suit's pattern had a weirder name than the last, like *tic weave* or *herringbone*.

"Sharkskin?!" I cried.

Dad was showing off this super-shiny blue suit with a matching hat, and talking with an overdone New York accent.

"It's just a name, kid," he replied. "It's not made-a sharks."

"I know," I bluffed.

"It's a blend. Wool, silk, mohair…"

"*What* hair?"

"*Fuhgeddaboutit!*"

And then I waited some more. I locked my hands together and rested my chin on them. This was our last weekend to practice my song before the

Innovation Conversation—and instead, we'd spent ninety minutes playing dress-up! I was having fun—Dad was always a lot of fun—but it sure didn't seem like "important business." This was goofy. Ridiculous.

Dad came out wearing one more suit, and the tailor followed a few steps behind. My mouth opened in a wide, toothy smile. "That's the one," I said.

His coat and vest were charcoal-colored, and underneath Dad wore a bold shirt that was blue like the ocean. He looked sharp, handsome, and mysterious—he looked like the Kidd on Keys.

"What do you say, sir?" asked the tailor.

Dad smoothed his lapels and checked himself out in the tall, three-sided mirror.

He glanced at me, and I nodded in encouragement. Then Dad faced the tailor. "I'm just…not sold on this," he said. "I just think today's not my day."

Dad changed back into his own clothes and the tailor gave us our coats. Dad tipped him, and then we left for the car empty-handed.

"Hey, next week," Dad said. "What time's your Innovation thing?"

"The first team performs at ten," I said. "We won't know the order we go 'til the day of, though."

"Then I'll be there at ten," he told me. Then he winked. "And dressed to the nines."

We reached the station wagon and climbed in— but my mind was still stuck at the tailor shop.

"Dad," I began, "didn't you like the suit I picked? You looked so cool."

He smiled. "I thought it was perfect."

I was totally confused. "Then why didn't you get it?"

Dad looked at me and grinned. "I never buy," he said. "I just like to try things on."

He started the car and we headed home. I really wanted to understand my dad, like Mr. Harvey said. But the more I learned about him, the harder it seemed to get.

Chapter Ten
Innovations, Conversations

"I'm so sorry!" I told Ella as I scratched behind her ears. "I wish you could come!"

The day was finally here—December fifteenth. It was just after sunrise, and in half an hour, we'd be heading up to a high school north of Pittsburgh for the first round of the Innovation Conversation. Mrs. Okocho was driving Momma and me, and since the host school was not far from where Dad lived, he was just going to meet us up there. My whole family would be cheering me on—everyone except for my pup, of course. I felt guilty that she was left out, especially since she'd had to listen to me practice every single night. I hoped that all the breakfast scraps I was feeding her would make up for it.

"How many sausage links has that been?" asked Momma.

"I'm just giving her the ends," I replied.

"You will make her tummy ache," Mrs. Okocho

cautioned as she scooped up some scrambled eggs with her toast. Momma had invited her to eat with us as a thank you for driving.

I swallowed my last bite and pushed my plate away. "May I go practice one last time?" I asked.

"Go ahead, Gifted and Talented," Momma said. "Not that you need it."

For the first time, I felt like Momma might actually be right. I knew "The Lonely Dog Blues" cold. And the rest of the team had stepped up, too. Our dress rehearsal on Thursday had gone so much better than last week. Maybe it was everybody's extra work, or maybe we all just felt surer of ourselves when we put on our costumes. I know that happened for me—even though my whole "costume" was really just a headband with a pair of felt dog ears glued to the ends. The way it changed me made me think of Dad and his weird suit-testing habit. Maybe he'd been onto something after all.

Ella followed me into my room, and I grabbed the dog-ear headband off my dresser. "You get a private preview," I told her.

My girl gave me the best compliment she could have: she sat right down to listen.

After we loaded the car, Mrs. Okocho drove us all the way up to a town called Moon. The high school there was hosting the Innovation Conversation in its gym.

We arrived right at nine—Mr. Harvey had told us to come early so we could get organized and practice. I lugged my dad's keyboard across the school parking lot with Momma and Mrs. Okocho at my sides.

"Sure you don't need a hand?" asked Momma.

"It's not so heavy," I replied. That wasn't totally true, but I was afraid that if I let go of the keyboard, the nervous tickle in my belly would come back.

When we entered the building, though, any plans I had to keep calm crumbled into dust. Mr. Harvey had told us there were a lot of schools competing, but this was too much to take in. The lobby and hallways were packed with team after team. Barely a few feet of space split each cluster. All of them were checking over props, practicing lines—near the corner, I even saw a pair of girls tap dancing in unison. "We don't have tap dancing," I told Momma.

"Don't worry about that," she said. "Let's just find your people."

By the time I spotted our team at the end of a hallway, Dad's keyboard case felt about three times heavier than when I'd pulled it out of the car. "If it isn't our playwright!" Mr. Harvey said. "Here, let me take that."

Mr. Harvey lifted the strap off my shoulder and I sighed in relief. He set it against a row of bright red lockers next to Darla, who was clapping a beat as Gautam practiced "Pesky Pete the Parakeet" for the four or five hundredth time.

"What time do we go on?" I asked.

"Eleven thirty-five," Mr. Harvey replied.

Perfect! I thought. That gave us plenty of time to practice, but it wasn't so late that we had to wait for hours and hours.

"What's the plan 'til then?" asked Momma. "Do the kids need any help?"

"I think we're all ready to rock," Mr. Harvey said. "I'd recommend finding a good seat in the gym. It's split with a divider. We're on the side with 'Tiger Pride' written on the wall."

I tapped Momma's elbow. "Can you call Dad and let him know where we'll be?"

"I'll tell him to find us in the front row," she replied. "Good luck!"

"It's *break a leg*," I corrected.

Mrs. Okocho inched past Momma and offered her hand to me. I took it and she gave me a firm shake. "Break your legs," she said.

Close enough, I thought with a grin. "Thanks, Mrs. O."

She and Momma worked their way back down the hall, weaving past a team of astronaut kids in puffy white snowsuits.

I turned around to find Darla standing half a foot behind me. "So," she said, "do you think we could practice just a little bit now?"

For the next hour, we huddled in the hall and held one last rehearsal. We worked through every bit of movement, every song, and every line of narration that came between. I'd added a narrator part to help explain what was happening—but also because everyone on the team had to participate and Russell refused to sing a single note.

A little before ten o'clock, the announcement speakers beeped loudly and a voice rang through the halls. "Round one of the Thirty-Third Annual Innovation Conversation will begin in ten minutes," it boomed. "Beginning teams, please head for the gymnasium and take your places."

I saw a team from our hall head out of sight. Other teams huddled together to have one last pep talk.

Mr. Harvey stepped into the middle of our group

and clapped his hands once. "All right, superstars, bring it in," he said. We formed a circle around him. "We need to meet back here at eleven-fifteen, on the button. I'll stay here to watch our props. If you want to stick around and practice more, let's respect the performers in the gym and do it very quietly. But personally…I think you guys are golden! I recommend that you relax, join your families, and enjoy some of the hard work the other teams have done."

I headed straight for the gym to check in with Momma. When I pulled open the doors, I spotted her and Mrs. Okocho in the front row of the bleachers like they'd promised. And they weren't alone, either.

"There she is!" Mrs. Jenkins cried. She was sitting beside Momma, applauding as I approached, and on her other side sat the rest of the Jenkins family.

"Thanks for coming," I told them.

"Like we'd miss our favorite neighbor's big stage debut," Mr. Jenkins said.

"I *told* you we'd be here," Ricky added, shaking his head.

I wasn't really focused on the Jenkinses, though. My eyes searched the rest of the gym—the basketball court, where the first team was setting up its backdrop, the upper rows of the bleachers, the entrances…

"Where's Dad?" I finally asked.

Momma shared a glance with Mrs. Okocho. "I couldn't reach him yet," Momma said. "He didn't answer his phone."

My heart began to rattle my ribs.

Mrs. Okocho smiled reassuringly. "He is probably driving here now and wants to be safe," she said.

"Can we call him again?" I asked. "Can we call right now?"

"Of course, sweetie," Momma replied.

But before we could leave the auditorium, a woman with horn-rimmed glasses and frosty hair stepped out onto the basketball court. She waved to the crowd with her wireless microphone. "Good morning, friends and families! My name is Edith Shapiro, head judge of…"

Momma took my arm and guided me to sit beside her. "We'll call again after this performance," she said.

"But Momma—"

"There's lots and lots of time," she promised. "You know how your father loves the last minute."

I nodded weakly. The head judge joined her partners at a table by the divider wall, and the first team began to perform. I barely even looked at their play. Instead, the whole time my mind raced through the different reasons Dad could be late.

Maybe he overslept.

Maybe he got mixed up and he's sitting on the other side of the divider.

Maybe he got another nosebleed and had to change his shirt.

Maybe he got lost on his way here.

Maybe he changed his mind—

I felt Momma shake my arm and applause sounded out around me. On the gym floor, the performers took a final bow. One kid was dressed as an explorer with a leather hat and a tan safari outfit, and four other kids were wrapped head-to-toe in Ace bandages. I felt really rude for zoning out during their whole play, so I clapped extra hard for them.

The second the applause died down, I led Momma out to the hallway so we could try Dad again.

"I'll do it," I insisted, and Momma handed me her phone.

I dialed Dad's number and waited. It never even rang—it just went straight to voicemail.

Momma could see it on my face. "I'm sorry, baby," she said, rubbing my back.

"Why is he doing this to me?" I demanded, my voice cracking.

Momma's gaze fell, and she just slightly shook her head.

But then she looked back up with calm eyes. "I'll do everything I can to get him here," she said. "I'll stand out here and call every other minute."

"What if he never turns on his phone?"

"Well…" Momma said, "his apartment isn't that far from here. If he doesn't answer in the next half hour, I'll send Mrs. Okocho there to get him."

I wiped a stray tear from the corner of my eye. "She'd do that?"

"Are you kidding?" Momma replied. "She'll tie him to her bumper if she has to."

A tiny smile fought its way onto my face.

"That's my beautiful girl," Momma said. "Just… try not to let it eat you up. This should be a great day for you. I'll take care of this."

I did my best to listen—but it was hard to stay in one place without looking at the clock every twenty seconds. So, I spent my time cycling between a few places. For a few minutes, I watched my teammates who were still rehearsing. When I got antsy, I went down the hall by myself and enjoyed all the craziness rushing by—the girl whose giant turtle shell costume kept getting caught on the locker handles, three boys who sprinted down the hall hefting a Styrofoam rocket ship above their heads.

In between all of that, I stopped by the gym to watch the other teams perform. The first time, I crammed myself in between Momma and Mrs. Okocho. But the second time I returned, Mrs. Okocho had stepped out.

"Did she really go to get Dad?" I asked.

Momma swept an arm around me, her grip strong and steady.

Mrs. Okocho was still gone when eleven-fifteen rolled around. "How far is it to Dad's house?" I asked Momma.

"From here? Twenty minutes, easy," she said. "When your team goes on, she will be here. Now go get 'em."

Momma kissed me on the head and the Jenkinses had me run past to give them each a high five—even Mrs. Jenkins, who practically stung my hand.

I took slow, full breaths as I joined the rest of the Talent Pool in the hall. Mr. Harvey was giving our team one last pep talk—how proud he was, how confident he felt about our chances. "You've already done the hard part," he told us. "You guys put together the funniest, most amazing, face-melting show in elementary world history. Now all you have to do is share it with everyone else."

Mr. Harvey held out his hand and we all put ours on top. The team did a cheer together, but I stayed quiet and made a wish. I probably don't have to say what it was.

We waited outside the gym doors for the team before us to clear out. I tried to peek through the small glass window, but I couldn't see the bleachers.

"Oh my gosh," Darla huffed, shifting the keyboard strap on her shoulder. "Take all day, please!"

"They're fine, we're fine," Mr. Harvey assured us.

When the last team had cleared away their props, a volunteer opened the doors for us. My eyes went straight for the bleachers. Momma and the Jenkinses were on their feet, and Mrs. Okocho was right there with them.

But no Dad.

I bit my lip to keep it from trembling. In the center of the floor, Donnie Yerba lined up a pair of easels from which he hung the backdrop we'd painted. Darla set up the keyboard and Russell took his place beside her to narrate. And I stood still, staring at Momma and Mrs. Okocho for an answer. Mrs. Okocho frowned and shook her head. Momma mouthed two words at me: *I'm sorry*.

"Come on," Gautam whispered, and he jostled me off to the sideline where the rest of the team had gathered.

The head judge, Miss Shapiro, read from a notecard to introduce us. "Presenting their original musical, *The Secret Lives of Pets*, I welcome, from the city of Pittsburgh, the students of Cedarville Elementary School!"

After a few seconds of cheering, Russell began his first lines. "On a day like today, in a house much like yours…"

When Russell finished, Darla struck a chord on the piano. Two girls wearing cat ears and matching black turtlenecks bounced out to sing the opening song, "Kitty Rock Anthem." They sang and danced, and the crowd cheered. But all I saw was the little gap between Momma and Mrs. Okocho where Dad should have been.

The show went on without a flaw. "Hamster" was a hit; Gautam managed to nail every word of "Pesky Pete the Parakeet"—and I couldn't have cared less.

Russell returned and spoke once again. "But not all of the pets had grand plans of mischief," he said. That was my cue. I gritted my teeth and went to my spot near the keyboard. "Tucked in a sad, little corner…" Russell said, "beneath a desk of solitude… lay a most loyal companion."

I knelt down beside Darla. I could see the keyboard case folded in half beneath Darla's chair. Staring up at me were those stitched-on words: *The Kidd on Keys*. I wanted to break my stupid dog-ear headband in half and run all the way home.

Russell held out his arms to the crowd. "A most loyal…and lonely…friend."

Darla played my song's little intro riff.

I couldn't remember a single word. I stared over at Darla, begging for help with my eyes.

She nodded a four count at me, and she played the intro one more time.

My mouth was so dry that it felt sealed shut. I could barely take a breath. I glimpsed my cheering section across from me—their smiles were fading as they watched me freeze. I wished I could just dissolve into the floor.

Darla played the intro once again. This time, though, I saw Ricky doing something. He was rifling through his coat. He pulled out a pair of drumsticks.

Darla played a fourth time, and Ricky tapped his legs on the two and the four. The intro played again, and this time Mr. Jenkins clapped along with his son.

My fear dropped away. But I didn't feel good underneath. I was furious. *They shouldn't be helping!* my brain screamed. *It shouldn't be them.*

Then something bizarre happened. In a flash, the words to my song came back, every single one. I began to sing.

No—I began to *roar.*

"*If you want to keep your smile,*
Then don't you look at me!"

I ripped through the song, swinging the notes as hard as I could, bending them like curveballs. The harder I pushed, though, the more it excited the crowd. The clapping spread to Mrs. Okocho and Momma, and then across the row, and then back to the top bleacher. Darla began to throw in more complicated note runs between each line.

"*Don't know where they went to be exact, but I just know they won't come back.*
I've got the left-me-all-alone-some, can't-even-pick-up-the-phone-some dog blues."

The bleachers exploded with applause. Ricky put his pinkies to his mouth and whistled. I hurried off to my teammates at the sidelines. "I feel sick…"

I whimpered, and I pushed straight past them and went into the hall.

I leaned against the lockers so I wouldn't fall over.

"Hey." I turned around and saw Ricky. "Are you okay?"

"Get away from me," I snapped.

Ricky looked totally puzzled. "What's going on?"

I stepped toward him. "Just go away, Ricky," I said, wiping my nose.

"Don't be embarrassed about freezing up," he said. "You were so awesome after."

Then I shoved him right in the chest.

"What is your problem?" he demanded.

"You are!" I yelled. "Go back to your perfect family and stay out of my life!"

Ricky's eyes got wet. Then he went back inside without another word. When the door closed, I sank down and scrunched against the lockers, and I bawled into my knees.

The gym doors reopened and I heard Momma rushing toward me. She wrapped her arms around me and I soaked her shoulder with my tears. "I'm here," she said.

And right then and there, she hooked an arm under my knees and lifted me off the ground like I was four years old again, like I was as light as a loaf of bread. "I'm taking you home," she told me.

I didn't argue. I couldn't find any words to say. A single thought flickered through my head, before it was gone, too. *I have the strongest Momma in the world.*

The phone woke me up like an alarm. As usual, Ella sprung from the foot of my bed and hurtled toward the kitchen to investigate. I didn't even shift under the covers. I just tilted my head and checked the clock—three in the afternoon. I couldn't believe I'd only been home for two hours. I felt like I'd slept half a day.

I heard Momma answer the phone. After a moment, she came to my door with it in her hand. Ella wiggled back in and hopped onto my bed.

I pushed myself up with my elbows. "Is it him?"

Momma shook her head. "Mr. Harvey," she replied. "He wanted to check on you."

Momma passed the phone to me. "Hello?"

"Hey there, playwright," Mr. Harvey said. "I hope your tummy's a little better."

Before we drove home from the Innovation Conversation, Mrs. Okocho had told him that I'd

gotten ill and needed to leave right away. Then she gathered Dad's keyboard for me as the team finished, and drove us straight home. Momma put the keyboard in her bedroom, because I couldn't stand to look at it.

"A little," I replied. Actually, my stomach felt grumbly—I'd skipped lunch and gone straight to bed when we got home.

"I'm glad," Mr. Harvey said. "Everybody was worried about you. Anyway, that's not the only reason I'm calling."

"What's the matter?" I asked.

"We just got our final score from the judges. Fourth place!"

I closed my eyes. We hadn't won. "Did we lose points because I left early?"

"What?" asked Mr. Harvey. "No way. Wait—this is *good* news! There were fifty-two teams there today. And the top five teams move on. We're going to the state round, Latasha!"

Different feelings rushed through me, too fast to even put them in order. I was proud, and excited, and energized…

"It's in Harrisburg, February ninth," Mr. Harvey continued. "We'll have plenty of time to make things perfect before then."

…And I was afraid. I couldn't go through another day like today. I just couldn't do it.

"What do you say?" he asked. "Are you ready to really buckle down?"

My answer shot out of me like it was trying to escape. "I quit."

Momma agreed to let me have alone time until dinner, on two conditions. The first: "After we eat, we're going to talk about Talent Pool." And the second: "You can't sleep the whole day away," she said. "Find something to do."

My usual choices were out. I didn't want to listen to music, and I couldn't find the right words to put in my journal. I tried writing an apology to Ricky for losing my temper, but everything I put down just seemed wrong. So instead, I did something I used to do a lot, which never failed to cheer me up—I read picture books to Ella.

Together, we caught up with our old friend Sam-I-Am; we learned what *really* happened between the Big Bad Wolf and the Three Little Pigs; and, of course, we did Ella's favorite thing—we let the wild rumpus start. But even though my bedroom door was wide open, my girl never ran out on me, not even for a second.

"You are the best, number one, A-plus little girl," I told her. She'd run out of gas and was now sprawled out, panting on my throw rug. Her surgery scar got itchy sometimes when she ran around, so I lightly swiped across the scar with my palm.

I heard a knock at our front door. Ella looked in its direction, but she didn't get up. "Uh-oh," I said, raising my eyebrows. "Okocho alert."

I didn't really mind, though. Story time had cheered me up and I owed her a thank you, anyway— she'd tried so hard to help. It wasn't her fault that Dad hadn't been home.

Momma opened the door and I waited for Mrs. Okocho's laugh. But that's not what I heard.

"You have a lot of nerve coming here," Momma hissed.

"I want to talk to her."

My face twisted and my stomach pulled tight.

I felt something rising inside me, but it wasn't tears this time. It was a fireball.

I sprung to my feet and went for my door. "You stay here," I told Ella. I closed her in the bedroom and charged for the kitchen.

"Do you realize what you did to her?" I heard

Momma say.

"I know, Steph. I know."

I turned the corner and saw Dad at the door. He and Momma looked at me.

"Where were you?" I growled.

"Kid," he began softly. "Things got really messed up, and—"

"—Where *were* you?"

"Latasha," Momma said, and she crossed toward me from the sink.

"I wasn't where I should have been," Dad replied. His gaze was so low that I could barely see his eyes. "I'm sorry."

"Apology not accepted!" I said. "Where were you?"

"I was—" Dad rubbed his cheeks. "I got kicked out of the band."

I opened my mouth, but I stayed silent. Dad grabbed a chair from the table and slumped onto it.

"Last night we had a gig," he said. "I missed part of the sound check. Joe lit into me, and I threw it right back at him. Maybe I crossed a line. I was stupid." He swallowed hard, his eyes flitting around the room until he settled back on Momma and me. "Joe tossed me. He sent me home. Except—I didn't go home, not until very late." He ran a hand through his wild hair.

"I lost my hat."

Dad looked like he'd shrunk a whole foot. "This morning," he continued, "nine-thirty, maybe? Your mother called me. I missed her, but it got me out of bed. I went to brush my teeth, and…I thought about Joe. And how I'd wrecked such a good thing." His lips smiled, but his eyes were dull. "So I hid. Turned off my phone, didn't answer my buzzer—not even when your landlady came by and tried to cuss the front door down. Because I couldn't think of facing you."

"I needed you there today," I said.

Dad nodded. "I know—and like I said, I'm sorry."

"But that doesn't fix it!" I shouted. "You made a promise. You promised you wouldn't forget me."

"I didn't forget," Dad insisted. "That's why I'm here. I didn't want you to think I up and forgot."

I folded my arms. "Oh, that's right," I said with a sharp scowl. "You thought really hard, and then you ditched me."

Dad tossed a hand up and let it fall. "What do you want me to say?" he asked, leaning toward me. "That I break my promises? That I'm a liar?"

I felt Momma grip my shoulders. "Don't talk to her that way," she warned.

Dad stood. "News flash, Latasha," he announced. "Your father is a loser. Okay? Are we clear? I mess things up. That's what I do."

I shrugged off Momma's hands. "But Daddy," I burst out, "if you keep messing up, how is Momma ever going to take you back?"

My words were a shock even to me. They'd just come out, before I could even think. Dad stared mutely. I heard Momma sniffle behind me.

"I…" Dad's eyes seemed foggy, like he'd been given a hard shake. "I don't want that."

The fire in me snuffed out and I went cold.

Dad looked at each of us. "I've got to…" He opened the door and rushed down the stairs. On the first floor, the front door slammed.

I finally knew my father. And all I could do was cry.

Chapter Eleven

The First Snow

"Only two more days until break," Momma said. "You're doing really well."

I closed my eyes so Momma couldn't see me rolling them. This was the fourth day straight that she'd given me a little pep talk out in front of my school, and all of her cheer was starting to annoy me. Only one person could make me feel better, and I hadn't heard a word from him since he'd run out of our kitchen. He hadn't even called about his keyboard.

"Just think," Momma went on. "Today and tomorrow here, and then you've got a whole eleven days off to play with Ella."

She brushed the fresh dusting of snow off my jacket. It was the first day we'd had snow on the ground, and Momma had been pointing out how beautiful everything looked the whole walk over. As if nothing was wrong at all.

"Remember the first time Ella went out in the snow?" she asked.

I remembered it perfectly. I'd taken her out back to go potty, but she was so confused by all the white on the ground. She'd done this goofy high-legged walk through it, like she was afraid of falling through—and she'd had no idea where she was allowed to pee.

That still wasn't enough to pull a smile out of me, though. I just wanted to disappear into the crowd of kids who were streaming in the front doors.

"Christmas, New Year's…" Momma said. "And then you've got a birthday right around the corner. Can you believe you'll be ten in a month?"

A month and a day, I thought with a sneer. *At least get the math right.*

But we'd argued enough times over the last few days. "Momma, I'm really cold," I said instead. "Can I go in now?"

"Oh! Sure thing," Momma said, adjusting the scarf around my neck. "I love you."

"You, too," I replied as I hurried off.

That morning, Miss Prooper kicked off social studies by reading a super-long list of Pennsylvania facts to us from a sheet of paper. I nodded along as she spoke, but really, I wasn't listening to a word. I was busy dreaming up a list of my own—a list about lunchtime and all the ways I could avoid it.

It was too bad, because Thursday was dinosaur chicken nugget day—but I couldn't deal with Darla or the other Talent Pool kids, and I *really* couldn't speak with Ricky. I was sure he hated me after how I'd treated him, and I was also pretty sure I deserved it.

For the first three days of the week, I'd used the same trick: I'd pretended I had a headache and got a cafeteria monitor to give me a pass to the nurse's office. That had worked out well—until the nurse mentioned calling Momma yesterday because of all of my headaches. So that was off the table.

It used to be that if I wanted a quiet lunch, I could go to Mr. Harvey's classroom. He always eats lunch at his desk so that students can use his classroom library—even past students, like me. But that was out now, too, for obvious reasons.

The library? I thought. *The band room?*

More than anything else, I wished that someone would just pick me up and take me out to lunch— that someone would pull up to the curb in their powder-blue station wagon and treat me one more time to the best french fries in the city. I screwed my eyes shut and hoped the idea would fade away.

"Miss Gandy?"

My eyes snapped open. Miss Prooper was peering at me over her reading glasses.

"Yes?" I replied, pasting a smile onto my face.

"Can you answer the question?" she asked.

I groaned to myself—this lady lived to catch kids who were zoning out. "Can…" I said. "Could you repeat it one more time?"

Miss Prooper sighed through her nose. "Can you tell us one nickname for the state of Pennsylvania?"

I gaped at Miss Prooper, unable to answer.

She arched a gray eyebrow. "The Blank State?"

I could feel all the eyes in the classroom shifting toward me. Finally Miss Prooper shook her head. "The Keystone State, the Quaker State, the Coal State, the Oil State…really, I just listed them five minutes ago."

Miss Prooper went to the chalkboard to write. Over her shoulder, she said, "Even our Gifted and Talented students need to pay attention, Miss Gandy."

A few kids around me snickered. I glowered at Miss Prooper's back. "I'm not Miss Gandy," I muttered. "That's my mother."

My teacher spun fiercely on her heel. "What was that?" she demanded.

I couldn't believe she'd heard me. "Nothing," I stammered.

Miss Prooper wedged her way down the aisle and stopped in front of me. "Are you absolutely sure?" she asked. I wanted to fold myself in half and hide inside my desk. "I'd love to hear—"

"Aw, come *on*!" someone interrupted.

I turned my chair with a screech. Dante was glaring at our teacher from the back row. "Leave her alone, Prooper-Scooper."

The whole room let out a long *ooooooh*.

"Quiet!" Miss Prooper barked.

I stared at Dante in disbelief, then back at her. Her mouth was open in a tiny little O. "Front office, now," she snarled. "The both of you."

I'd been to our In-School-Suspension room once before, last year. It wasn't like today, though. I'd just been taking something to a friend—I hadn't had to stay.

That was what Dr. DeSoto decided when Dante and I got to the office. She gave us a lecture about showing respect to our teachers and then she escorted us down to I.S.S.

At least I got out of lunch, I thought.

There were already two other kids in different corners of the room when we arrived. Dr. DeSoto gave instructions about us to Miss Schneider, who teaches gym and runs I.S.S. "They're here 'til the final bell," our principal said, and then she left.

Miss Schneider refolded her newspaper. "Have a seat," she told us.

As soon as we'd sat, I asked Dante the question I'd had ever since his outburst. "What were you thinking?" I whispered.

"I said 'have a seat,'" Miss Schneider reminded us, "not 'have a chat.'"

I frowned. I didn't say anything more, but I looked at Dante for an answer.

Dante pulled a spiral notebook from his backpack. He wrote something on a page and turned it so I could see. His note read, *You've been sad.*

I glanced at Miss Schneider. She was hunched over her desk, working on the crossword page. I leaned over to Dante's notebook and wrote back. *Who says I'm sad?*

Dante tapped himself on the chest. Then he wrote, *I tried to help you.*

I snatched the notebook from him. *How is <u>this</u> help?* I scribbled.

Dante gently took it back. *My plan didn't work*, he wrote. *Sorry.*

What plan?

To get sent here, Dante wrote.

I scrunched my eyebrows—each thing that kid wrote was more confusing than the last.

He added on the next line: *I thought she'd just punish me. Not us.*

I closed my eyes in frustration. Who on Earth would actually *want* to get punished?

Dante noticed my expression and wrote some more. When he finished, he tore out the page and handed it to me. *If you get in trouble,* the note read, *your mom will be mad. But it's okay for me. My parents don't care.*

I tried to look Dante in the eye, but he just studied the scratches on the top of his desk.

When the final bell rang, we were free to go—and free to talk.

"Thanks again for sticking up for me," I told Dante as we zipped up our coats.

"Don't sweat it, Gandy," he replied. Then he turned to face me. "Actually, do me a favor. Talk to Jenkins, would you?"

My whole body tensed up. "I don't know," I said. I went out to the hallway, which was jammed with kids in bulky winter gear.

Dante hurried after me. "You have to," he pleaded. "For real, that dude has been bumming me out all week! Moping around like a little girl." He winced. "No offense."

"No offense," I agreed. We stopped in the front foyer. "You know, you're a good friend."

Dante just shrugged.

I was going to ask him if he needed a ride home, but I got interrupted by a loud voice.

"Latasha! Hey!"

I turned and my stomach dropped down to my knees. Darla and Gautam were running toward me with big smiles on their faces.

"Long time, no see!" Darla said. "Are you feeling better?"

I wasn't anymore, but Gautam chimed in before I could say anything. "We heard you cursed out Miss Prooper in class!"

"I didn't!" I protested. "Dante and I just got busted for talking back."

"Oh," Gautam said.

"And it was really just me," Dante added.

Darla glanced at the two boys with a smirk. "Anyway," she said, "we're getting Yoo-Hoos from the vending machine before Talent Pool. You want to come?"

I wondered for a second why they were even talking to me, but then realized: *They don't know that*

I quit. Then I realized something else: *I'm going to have to tell them I quit.* And that meant I'd have to tell them the whole messy story of *why* I quit.

Instead, I bolted out the front door.

"Hey!" Dante called after me.

Mrs. Okocho's Oldsmobile was already idling by the yellow curb. I jumped into her car and slammed the door shut. Instead of pulling away, Mrs. Okocho looked over at me with concern. "The principal called your mama," she said. "This is not like you."

"Please just drive," I huffed.

"Just this once," I moaned at Ella, "stay down!" I usually loved my pup's dancing hellos, but I'd had the worst day of a lousy week, and I was in for an awful night, too, once Momma got home. I didn't want to fight with Momma—but I didn't think I'd be able to stop myself, either.

I fumbled with Ella's leash, trying to clip it on. "I can't take you for potty 'til you settle," I grumbled.

My fingers hooked under her collar, but Ella spun in a circle and wrenched my wrist. "Ow!" I shouted, bolting to my feet. I gave the kitchen floor a room-rattling stomp. "Ella Fitzgerald Gandy!"

Her tail dropped and she galloped away to my bedroom. I chased after her, just in time to see her scramble under my bed. "Ella, you come out right now," I snapped.

The phone rang in the kitchen.

I turned my head toward the doorway, then back to Ella. She just watched me from the shadows. It made me feel like a monster.

The phone kept ringing. "This is not over, pup," I warned, and I stalked out of the room.

I yanked the phone off the receiver. "Hello."

"Latasha," Mrs. Okocho said on the other end.

"I know, I know," I replied. "I'm being loud up here. I'll stop."

"Latasha," she repeated in a sharp tone. "Will you please come join me for tea? I insist."

I knew that when Momma was at work, Mrs. Okocho was the boss. But I wasn't about to pretend that I liked it.

"I don't know," I told her. "I think I'd rather have *coffee*."

Mrs. Okocho set her silver tea tray on the dining room table. "Coffee is a drink for fun," she replied coolly. "Serious times call for tea."

Whatever, I thought.

Mrs. Okocho filled our cups from her teapot and sat down. "You know," she said, stirring in a lump of sugar, "you are right to be angry with him."

That made me pause. "Thank you," I said. I grabbed the plastic bear full of honey and dribbled some into my tea.

"For a long while," she said, "I was very angry with Mr. Okocho."

I waited for her to continue. Mrs. Okocho rarely mentioned her husband—all I really knew was that he had died some time before we moved in. "On the day he passed," she said, "he asked that I fry plantains for lunch. These are a fruit, like a banana. I did not have any in my kitchen, so I walked to the market. It was a beautiful day. A good day to start a garden. I bought the plantains, and hibiscus leaves as well, to make a punch. When I returned…he had gone to sleep."

I had no idea what I should say.

"My heart was shattered, of course," she said. "But I was angry as well. I hated him for leaving me without even a warning."

The story made me sad and frustrated at the same time. "But it's not like he wanted to go," I replied. "It's not the same!"

"I know it is not the same," Mrs. Okocho admitted.

I yanked a napkin from the holder on the table. "Then why'd you even tell me all that?" I asked, rubbing the corners of my eyes.

"Because, child," she replied, "sometimes people we love very much…they leave us. And we do not get any choice in the matter."

I snorted—as if I needed to be told that.

Mrs. Okocho clasped her hands and set them on the table. "But there is something we can choose," she said. "How we treat those who are still here."

I gave the ceiling a long look. "I think I owe some apologies," I said.

Mrs. Okocho smiled. "Drink your tea first," she told me. "Ella will wait for you."

I obeyed and took a sip. "It's not her I'm worried about."

"What a pleasant surprise!" Mrs. Jenkins said. "Ricky's out back."

After I'd made up with Ella—which only took

about a dozen treats and five minutes of belly-rubs—
it was time to get to the hard stuff. Mrs. Jenkins led
me across the house toward the back door. "Your
show was wonderful," she told me.

"Thank you," I replied. "I'm sorry that we
disappeared after. That was my fault."

Mrs. Jenkins shook her head. "No," she said with
a hint of a smile.

Outside, Ricky was bundled up in a dark blue
snowsuit. "Let's run, Ham!" he shouted as he dove
past his dog and slid across the frozen ground. If
Hamlet was impressed, he sure didn't show it.

I opened the door and stepped out. "Don't break
a drumstick," I called to them.

Ricky flopped on his back and looked at me.
Hamlet, to my surprise, stood up and walked over.
He went past me to the window, leaving smeary nose
prints on the glass. I realized who he was looking for.
"It's just me today," I told him, patting his head.

Ricky trudged over to me. I pointed out to the
ground where he'd been sliding. "How'd you get it so
icy?" I asked. "Garden hose?"

"What do you want, Latasha," he said flatly.

"I was really mean to you," I said.

"Yeah, you were," he agreed.

"And it wasn't fair."

"When are you going to tell me something I don't know?"

"I will, if you quit sassing me!" I snapped.

Ricky bit back a grin. "This is the worst apology ever," he said.

I nodded wearily. "Can we go inside?" I asked. "It might take a while."

We went back in, and once Ricky had changed into regular clothes, we sat in the living room near the fireplace. And I told him everything—even the embarrassing stuff, like how I'd been jealous of him, and how I thought my dad would fix everything, and how I couldn't have been more wrong. "He doesn't even want to be my dad," I whispered.

Ricky was leaning back against Hamlet on the floor, just listening. I don't think he knew what to say.

"Anyway," I went on. "I'm really sorry for how I treated you."

"Yeah," Ricky said. "I'm really sorry, too."

"What are you sorry for?" I asked.

Ricky furrowed his brow. "I don't really know," he replied. "I just feel sorry."

"You don't have to be sorry," I said. "You didn't do anything bad."

He sat up straight. "I didn't?"

I shook my head.

"Wow," he mused. "That's a first."

That made me chuckle. I pushed myself to my feet. "I'd better get going," I said.

"Do you have to?" asked Ricky.

"Momma will hit the roof if she comes home and I'm not there," I said. "I've got another long talk coming. And I know just how it's going to start, too."

"Latasha Esther Gandy?" asked Ricky.

"Big time."

When Momma got home, she sure didn't let me down. She practically bellowed my name, and then she went off with a bunch of those questions that weren't really questions. "What has gotten into you? What were you thinking?"

For the first few seconds of scolding, I was itching to raise my voice back. But I thought of Mrs. Okocho—and, weirdly enough, Dante—and waited it out. Once Momma had cooled off, I explained what had happened in school, and why.

I still had to write an apology to Miss Prooper, but Momma was more understanding than I'd expected. "You can come home and vent when you need to," she told me, "but you can't mouth off to your teachers, not ever."

I nodded. "Can we go in early tomorrow, then?" I asked. "I don't want to give my note to her in front of the whole class."

"Sure thing," she replied. "I'll even come in with you, if you want."

"Maybe," I said.

Momma smiled at me. "Everything will be fine," she told me. "You'll see."

That reminded me of something. "Momma," I began. "Don't take this the wrong way."

She tilted her head and waited.

"Please don't give me any more pep talks," I sighed. "They really get on my nerves."

Momma clutched my hand. "Deal."

Chapter Twelve
Family-Only

The next day, I skipped lunch again—but not to hide out.

"What can I do for you?" asked Mr. Harvey, sliding aside his carton of Chinese food.

I stepped into his classroom, ready to beg if I had to. "I don't want to let the Talent Pool down," I said. "Can I…" I was so nervous that I couldn't think of the right word. "Can I un-quit?"

Mr. Harvey gave me a knowing grin and jammed his chopsticks into the carton. "Un-quit?" he said. "What makes you think I ever let you quit in the first place?"

Then, just a couple of hours later, winter break began. And one by one, my days got better. I passed the time doing crafts with Mrs. Okocho and taking Ella across to Ricky's for play dates with Hamlet. And even though work tired her out, each night Momma stayed up with me to watch a movie, work on a puzzle, or have me read aloud to her.

I still stumbled sometimes when I felt extra-lonely—like on Christmas, when I got mad and tried to bend my *Tough Ladies* mix CD in half. I didn't realize that CDs don't bend—they shatter and leave a glittery mess all over the carpet. I was just lucky that Ella didn't try to eat any of it.

Mostly, though, I felt okay, as long as I stayed away from things that made me miss Dad. Some things were easy to avoid, like the Dirty O. Other things took more effort. The day school got back in session, I moved Dad's keyboard out of the house and into Mr. Harvey's supply closet so I'd never have to see it outside of Talent Pool practice.

But one thing was impossible to dodge.

"What do you mean, you don't want to do anything for your birthday?" asked Momma. "You're going into double digits!"

"I already said why," I answered. If there was any one day that made me think of Dad, it was my birthday. I could remember every card he'd sent me—before these past few months, my birthday had been the only day I felt like I had a father.

"I know," Momma said. "But…I want to throw you a real party. We can finally afford one."

Just before New Year's, Momma had done something huge—she'd made the final payment on Ella's surgery! We'd walked over to Dr. Vanderstam's and delivered it personally, then we'd stopped for a slice at Pizza Franco on the way home.

But even Momma's party offer couldn't sway me. "January twenty-first," I said testily, "is going to be a normal, boring day."

"Technically, this would be on the nineteenth," Momma said. "The Saturday before."

I lowered my brow at her.

"C'mon," she said, sliding closer to me on the couch. "We've got a week to plan the perfect party. I'll make sure you have a great time. Pizza, cake, games, all of your friends—"

"—Momma," I interrupted. "You're pep-talking."

"Well," she replied. "Forgive me for thinking that the day you came into the world is worth celebrating."

I sighed loudly.

"Look," Momma said. "You can't just pretend you don't have a birthday. How about we do something small? No streamers, no party hats…something family-only."

I closed one eye as I thought it over. "Can we have cookie cake?" I asked.

Momma's face lit up. "That's my girl."

The morning of our family-only party, I came out of the shower to find Momma fussing with something on Ella's head. "Relax, pup…"

"Momma!" I complained, yanking away the towel that was wrapped around my hair. "You said no party hats!"

Momma turned toward me. "Come on, she looks adorable."

Actually, with the party hat cocked forward on her brow, Ella looked a bit like a unicorn. That is, until she whipped the hat off her head, grabbed it in her teeth, and dashed for my room.

Momma and I shared a grin. "It was worth a try," she said.

Around eleven, we opened my presents. Momma only got me one thing, but it was the perfect thing—an e-reader!

"Now you can carry as many books as you want," she said.

"Thank you, thank you, thank you!" I squealed.

From Ella, I got a new notebook and a really nice fountain pen in a clear plastic case. But I liked the note that came with it best of all. It said, in handwriting that only looked a little like Momma's: *Please do not let me eat this pen. I know I will try.*

After Momma and I spent some time searching online for e-books, we heard a knock at the door. Ella scrambled off in an instant, but before Momma or I could get up, the door opened. "Hi, hello, good morning!" Mrs. Okocho shouted.

"You said we were doing family-only today," I told Momma with a grimace.

"What?" she asked. "Mrs. O isn't family?"

I opened my mouth to argue, but it was actually a pretty good point.

"Aiy! Down!" Mrs. Okocho cried. "Down, you fiend!"

Momma and I hustled to the kitchen and bribed Ella away before she could lick our landlady to death. Mrs. Okocho wiped her cheek with a shudder, and then approached me. She handed over a dense, box-shaped object wrapped in pink paper.

"I hope you will be surprised," she said. She leaned in close. "It is a thesaurus."

I hefted the heavy gift in my hands. "I'm very surprised," I told her.

Momma grilled mozzarella sandwiches for lunch, and then she pulled my cake out of the fridge. "The bakery said we should let it warm up a little first," she told us. She joined us at the table. "What do you want to do until then?"

"Latasha," Mrs. Okocho said excitedly, "now that you are ten years, I could teach to you my favorite card game. Have you ever heard of blackjack?"

I had! "Oh, I don't know about that," Momma cut in.

"We will not play for money!" Mrs. Okocho promised. Then, with a wink she added, "Well, no more than you can afford to lose, ha-ha!"

I grinned widely. Momma and Mrs. Okocho argued back and forth about blackjack until they were interrupted by another knock at the door.

"Latasha," Momma said over Ella's jumpy racket, "would you get that?"

I could tell she knew who it was. Like I was tearing off a bandage, I closed my eyes, gripped the doorknob, and yanked it open.

"Happy birthday!" yelled the Jenkinses.

Ella leaped into my back and knocked me right into them. Thankfully, Mr. and Mrs. Jenkins each caught one of my arms before I could totally topple over.

"Good gravy," Mr. Jenkins said as they filed into the apartment.

"Oh my gosh, Dad," Ricky scoffed. He handed me another box-shaped gift, this one lighter than Mrs. Okocho's. "This is from us, plus Ham."

I gripped the present firmly. My eyes drifted to Momma's smiling face. I didn't know what to say.

Mrs. Jenkins stepped beside me. "Your mother said you wanted a family-only day," she explained. "But I figured—well, you're part of our family. So here we are."

I looked around the kitchen. I'd never seen it so crowded. And I wanted to hug every person in it. But how would there ever be enough time to do it right?

Ricky's voice snapped me out of my trance. "You want to open that thing?" he asked.

"Ricardo," Mr. Jenkins warned.

"No worries," I said, shaking my head. I tore away the paper to reveal a photograph in a wood frame. It gave me a lump in my throat.

"What is it?" asked Mrs. Okocho.

I showed her the picture. It was a fall day on Graham Street. Ricky and I were standing on the sidewalk, flashing million-watt smiles. Hamlet sat, expressionless, at Ricky's side. At my feet, a panting tripod dog splayed out on the concrete. Inked in calligraphy on the mat holding the photo were two words: *Best Buddies*.

After Mrs. Okocho and the moms got their *awws* out of the way, it was time for cake. Everyone sang "Happy Birthday" and I blew out my candles in a single breath. Then Momma watched as I used a big knife to make the first cut.

"Did I surprise you?" she asked.

I turned to her. "I thought this was a no-secrets house," I replied.

She placed a hand on each of my cheeks and kissed my forehead. "Let's call today an exception."

Each guest took a cut of cake and moved into the

living room to sit.

After everyone had gotten a piece, I noticed there was still a quarter-cake left.

"We can freeze it," Momma assured me.

"Actually," I said, looking at the leftovers, "can I call someone else to come over? Another friend?"

Momma nodded, pleased. "Absolutely," she said.

"They might need a ride," I added.

"I'm sure someone will help."

I sprang to the living room doorway. "Hey, Ricky," I called in. "What's Dante's number?"

It turned out on Monday that Momma had one last surprise for me. When I walked out of school, I found her waiting for me at the curb. "I traded half a shift," she told me. "I wasn't about to let you spend the afternoon alone on your birthday. Get your earmuffs on and we'll start walking."

As we trekked home, I told Momma about how great the day had been. "Miss Prooper didn't mention my birthday," I explained, "but everybody else did. Darla and the Talent Pool kids sang to me at lunch, and Mr. Harvey came by and gave me a cupcake!"

"That was very thoughtful of him," Momma said.

"I saved it for dessert tonight. It's vanilla with strawberry icing."

"You might want to eat it now," she suggested. "Mrs. Okocho's been cooking today. A stew or something. It's very…"

"Malodorous?" I asked.

Momma's cheeks dimpled. "You've cracked your thesaurus, I see."

When we reached our porch, I noticed that the lid of our mailbox was open. When I gave it a closer look, my heart began to beat in double time.

A thick manila envelope was stuffed inside the box. I pulled it out and shook it to hear the coins rattle inside. Momma looked at it warily. "I could open that for you," she said, "if you want."

I flipped Dad's envelope in my hands. "I'll be okay," I said.

I rushed up the stairs. I was so eager to open the envelope that I barely noticed the weird aromas wafting from under Mrs. Okocho's door.

I unlocked our door and pushed past Ella to the kitchen table. I tore the envelope open and shook the change and Dad's note out onto the table. I looked at the note. My eyebrows creased in confusion.

Momma came in and knelt next to Ella, rubbing her belly to settle her down. Honestly, I could have used some of that. "What did he write?" she asked.

"'From the Kidd to his kid—happy tenth,'" I read. "'Here's to having one more chance.'"

"That's weird," Momma said.

I looked at the coins on the table. Ten pennies, ten nickels, ten dimes, ten quarters—no dollars. I shook the envelope again and realized it wasn't empty. I removed the paper hiding inside, but it wasn't cash. It was ten one-dollar scratch lottery tickets.

I tossed them onto the table. What was this supposed to mean? That he wanted another chance from me? That he wanted me to forgive him? Or was it just about the scratch tickets, and nothing more? I had half a mind to leave Dad's note and the tickets on my bedroom floor and let Ella "play" with them. I saw her near the corner now, sniffing at the heating vent. She must have caught scent of Mrs. Okocho's strange cooking.

I realized what I could do. "Momma, I'm running downstairs for a minute."

"Are you sure?" asked Mrs. Okocho.

I wasn't at all—but I didn't want time to change my mind. "You scratch," I said, "and I'll eat."

Mrs. Okocho sat at her table, my scratch tickets on her place mat, a silver dollar in hand. I sat across from her. And waiting in front of me was a steaming bowl of Mrs. Okocho's funky stew. It was a thick, globby red with vegetables and chunks of some kind of steak in it. It smelled like lemon and pepper—and gym class.

"We start together," Mrs. Okocho said. She set down the tickets and raised her silver dollar. "Do not worry. I took out the bones."

That almost sent me running out of the room. But then Mrs. Okocho scratched her first ticket, so I held my breath and spooned a bite into my mouth. I chewed the meat and vegetables, and when there was nothing left to chew, I swallowed it. The taste was—

"This is really…good?!" I exclaimed, completely baffled.

"Do you taste the garlic?" asked Mrs. Okocho, tossing a scratch ticket aside.

I took another bite. "Yeah, I do!" I said, licking my lips. "I couldn't smell it before."

I ate another few bites, searching for a nice chunk of that tasty steak. I actually thought I might have a second serving.

"Yes," she said, "the taste is much better than the smell. That is the trouble with goat stew."

I looked over at her. "With what now?"

"The goat meat," Mrs. Okocho said. "It has an odor."

My spoon clattered into my dish. "I just ate a goat?" I cried.

Mrs. Okocho chuckled. "Come now," she said, holding her fingers a few inches apart. "You ate that much of a goat."

"I just ate a cute little goat," I moaned. I couldn't even look at my bowl. Why had I gone through with this dopey idea?

"And, I might add, you loved it," Mrs. Okocho said.

I didn't look at her.

"Cows are cute," she said with a frown. "So are pigs…in the right light."

I peeked down at my bowl.

"It was good, no?" asked Mrs. Okocho.

"All right," I admitted. "It was."

"Then there is no problem," she said. She scratched her last ticket. "Bah! Not a winner in the bunch! This is why I prefer the blackjack."

I slowly ate another bite of my stew. It had no right to taste this good. "Can I…bring some of this up to Ella?"

"Oh, my stew is fit for a dog!" Mrs. Okocho

exclaimed. "What a compliment to the chef!"

"Sorry," I said.

"Why not share some with your mama instead?" she asked.

Mrs. Okocho made me a Tupperware of goat stew and I carried it up the stairs. "What's that you've got there?" asked Momma. She was spreading some peanut butter down a celery stalk.

"Early dinner!" I said. "It's from Mrs. Okocho. I tried it, and it is awesome."

Momma looked at me like I'd turned into a toad. "You tried her foot-stinky stew?" she asked.

"It tastes totally different," I insisted. I heard tapping at my feet. Ella had snuck up like a three-legged ninja and sat there, her happy tail whacking the floor. "Ella wants some."

"Ella eats dryer sheets," Momma retorted.

"Come on," I said. "Can't you be brave like me?"

Momma cracked a knowing grin. "Get me a spoon," she said.

I fetched one from the drawer while Momma opened the Tupperware. She ducked back at the smell and cried, "Good golly, Miss Molly!"

I crossed my arms.

"If it wasn't your birthday…" Momma said, and she took a bite.

I watched her face change just like mine had. "Wow," she said.

She ate some more, nodding all the while. She picked out a piece of goat meat for Ella. "A treat for the pup!" she announced, and she fed it to her.

"Wasn't I right?" I asked.

"You were," Momma admitted.

Ella circled around the table and sat beside her again.

"What do you know," Momma said, "a new dog!" She gave Ella a carrot slice and took another bite.

Momma tapped her spoon against the side of the Tupperware. "It's a little different," she said, "but this right here is the best beef stew that I have ever tried."

I watched Momma eat all the stew and scrape the very last spoonfuls of sauce. Once or twice, I came right up to the edge of telling her that she was not eating beef. We are, after all, a no-secrets family. But like Momma'd told me, there are exceptions. Sometimes, it's simply better not to know.

The End

Acknowledgements

Such little space, so many to thank—thank you to my Lincoln Learning Solutions colleagues, who've been as supportive as can be as I wrote, traveled, and spoke to students.

Jenn, Debbie, Ang, Vinnie, and the rest of my draft readers: thanks for assuring me this book was going somewhere.

I had a big assist from my various online writing communities. Thanks to the members of #kidlitchat, #mglitchat, and, of course, the #nerdybookclub crew. Writing can be a solitary affair, but you all helped to keep it lively.

I'm grateful to many inspiring teachers—some from the past, and some whom I've only recently met. Thank you, Sharon, Milan, Jim, Hilary, Jane, Melissa, and Donalyn, and thanks especially to Colby, one of my biggest Latasha boosters, and who first planted the possibility that I should write this sequel.

Most important of all, thanks to every young person whose school I visited. Thank you, kids, for your boundless energy, your love of reading, and your audible excitement every time I mentioned this novel. If you hadn't wanted it, I might never have finished it.

About the Author

Michael Scotto is the author of the Tales of Midlandia picture book series, as well as the middle-grade novels *Postcards from Pismo* and *Latasha and the Little Red Tornado.* He currently lives with his wife and their very naughty dog in Pittsburgh, PA, a mere three miles from Latasha's home. For his contributions as an advocate for youth literacy and creative thought, Michael was honored in 2011 by *Pittsburgh Magazine* and PUMP as one of the "Pittsburgh 40 Under 40." *Latasha and the Kidd on Keys* is his third novel.

About the Illustrator

Evette Gabriel is a contributing artist for the Tales of Midlandia picture book series, as well as the illustrator of the middle-grade novel *Latasha and the Little Red Tornado.* Evette has worked at the *Pittsburgh Tribune-Review* as an editorial staff illustrator and continues to work in the editorial and children's markets. She currently lives with her husband, son, and two feline companions in Pittsburgh, PA.